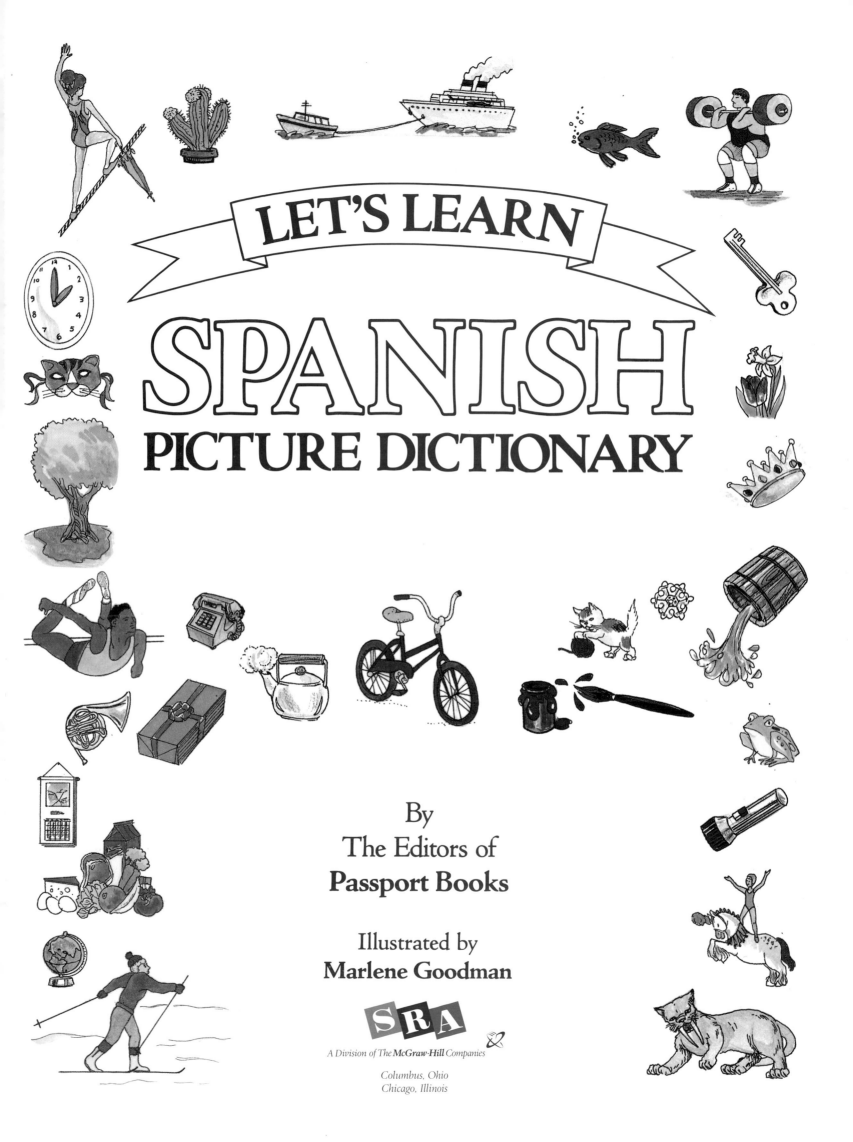

LET'S LEARN
SPANISH
PICTURE DICTIONARY

By
The Editors of
Passport Books

Illustrated by
Marlene Goodman

SRA

A Division of The **McGraw-Hill** Companies

Columbus, Ohio
Chicago, Illinois

Welcome to the *Let's Learn Spanish* Picture Dictionary!

Here's an exciting way for you to learn more than 1,500 Spanish words that will help you speak about many of your favorite subjects. With these words, you will be able to talk in Spanish about your house, sports, outer space, the ocean, and many more subjects.

This dictionary is fun to use. On each page, you will see drawings with the Spanish and English words that describe them underneath. These drawings are usually part of a large, colorful scene. See if you can find all the words in the big scene, and then try to remember how to say each one in Spanish. You will enjoy looking at the pictures more and more as you learn more Spanish.

You will notice that almost all the Spanish words in this book have **el, la, los,** or **las** before them. These words simply mean "the" and are usually used when you talk about things in Spanish.

At the back of the book, you will find a Spanish-English Glossary and Index and an English-Spanish Glossary and Index, where you can look up words in alphabetical order, and find out exactly where the words are located in the dictionary. There is also a section that explains how you say Spanish sounds as well as pronunciation guides that will help you say each Spanish word correctly.

This is a book you can look at over and over again, and each time you look, you will find something new. You'll learn the Spanish words for people, places, and things you know, and you may even learn some new words in English as you go along!

Library of Congress Cataloging-in-Publication Data
is available from the United States Library of Congress.

Illustrations by Terrie Meider
7. Clothing; 15. People in our Community; 18. Sports; 28. Colors;
29. The Family Tree; 30. Shapes; 31. Numbers; 32. Map of the World.

www.sra4kids.com

SRA/McGraw-Hill

A Division of The McGraw·Hill Companies

Copyright © 1991 by SRA/McGraw-Hill.

Send all inquiries to:
SRA/McGraw-Hill
P.O. Box 812960
Chicago, IL 60681

Printed in the United States of America.

ISBN 0-8442-7558-1

2 3 4 5 6 7 8 9 RRW 07 06 05 04 03 02

Table of Contents
Índice de materias

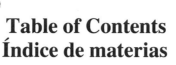

1. Our Classroom **Nuestra aula**
2. Our House **Nuestra casa**
3. The Kitchen/The Utility Room **La cocina/El cuarto de auxilio**
4. The Attic **El desván**
5. The Four Seasons (Weather) **Las cuatro estaciones (El tiempo)**
6. At the Supermarket **En el supermercado**
7. Clothing **La ropa**
8. In the City **En la ciudad**
9. In the Country **En el campo**
10. In a Restaurant **En un restaurante**
11. The Doctor's Office/The Dentist's Office **La oficina del médico/ La oficina dcl dentista**
12. The Barber Shop/Beauty Shop **La peluquería de caballeros y señoras**
13. The Post Office/The Bank **El correo/El banco**
14. At the Gas Station **En la gasolinera**
15. People in Our Community **Las personas de nuestra comunidad**
16. Going Places (Transportation) **El transporte**

17. The Airport **El aeropuerto**
18. Sports **Los deportes**
19. The Talent Show **El espectáculo**
20. At the Zoo **En el jardín zoológico**
21. At the Circus **En el circo**
22. In the Ocean **En el mar**
23. Space **El espacio**
24. Human History **La historia de la humanidad**
25. The Make-Believe Castle **El castillo de ficción**
26. The Mouse Hunt (Prepositions and Adjectives) **A la caza del ratón (Preposiciones y adjetivos)**
27. Action Words **Palabras de acción**
28. Colors **Los colores**
29. The Family Tree **El árbol genealógico**
30. Shapes **Las formas**
31. Numbers **Los números**
32. A Map of the World **Un mapamundi**

Spanish-English Glossary and Index
    How to Say the Words in Spanish

English-Spanish Glossary and Index

1. Our Classroom   Nuestra aula

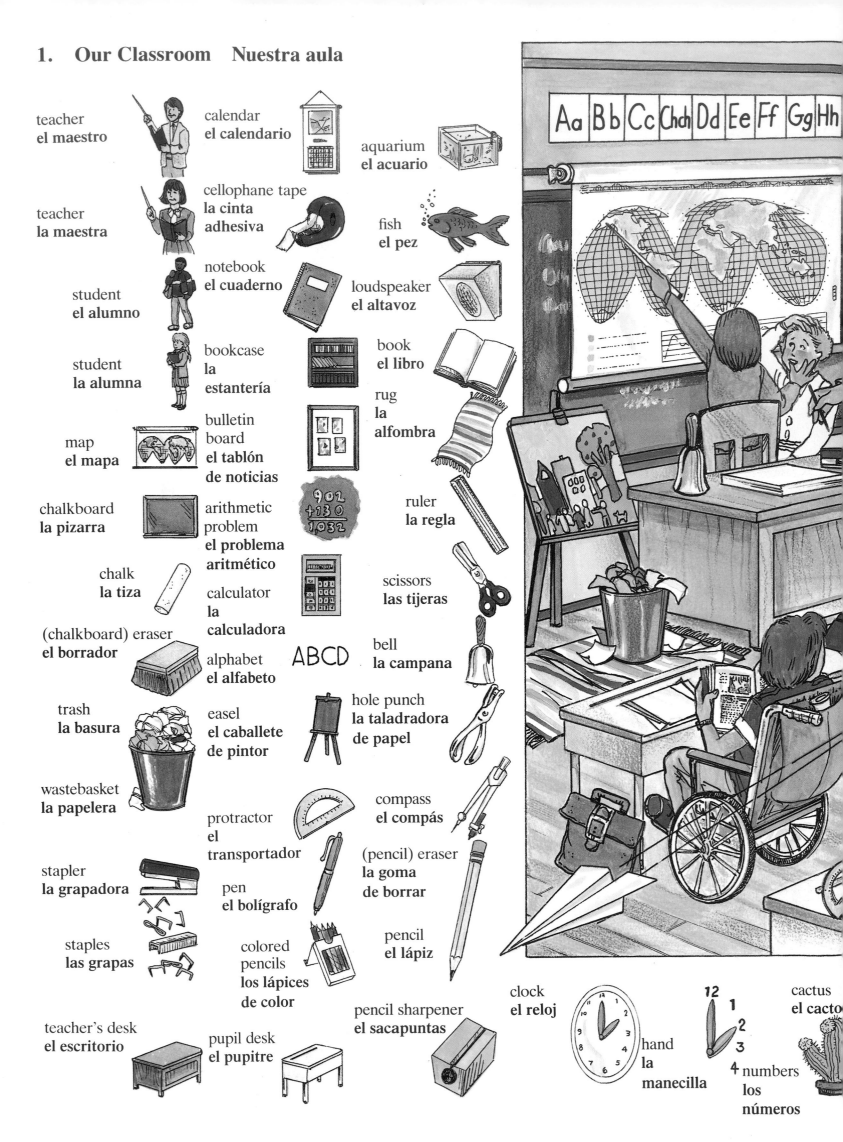

teacher
el maestro

teacher
la maestra

student
el alumno

student
la alumna

map
el mapa

chalkboard
la pizarra

chalk
la tiza

(chalkboard) eraser
el borrador

trash
la basura

wastebasket
la papelera

stapler
la grapadora

staples
las grapas

teacher's desk
el escritorio

calendar
el calendario

cellophane tape
**la cinta
adhesiva**

notebook
el cuaderno

bookcase
**la
estantería**

bulletin
board
**el tablón
de noticias**

arithmetic
problem
**el problema
aritmético**

calculator
**la
calculadora**

alphabet
el alfabeto

ABCD

easel
**el caballete
de pintor**

protractor
**el
transportador**

pen
el bolígrafo

colored
pencils
**los lápices
de color**

pencil sharpener
el sacapuntas

pupil desk
el pupitre

aquarium
el acuario

fish
el pez

loudspeaker
el altavoz

book
el libro

rug
**la
alfombra**

902
+130
1032

ruler
la regla

scissors
las tijeras

bell
la campana

hole punch
**la taladradora
de papel**

compass
el compás

(pencil) eraser
**la goma
de borrar**

pencil
el lápiz

Aa Bb Cc Chch Dd Ee Ff Gg Hh

clock
el reloj

hand
**la
manecilla**

12
1
2
3
4 numbers
los
números

cactus
el cacto

plant
la planta

glue
la cola

globe
**el globo
terráqueo**

picture
el cuadro

paint
la pintura

paintbrush
el pincel

paper
el papel

crayon
el creyón

2. Our House
Nuestra casa

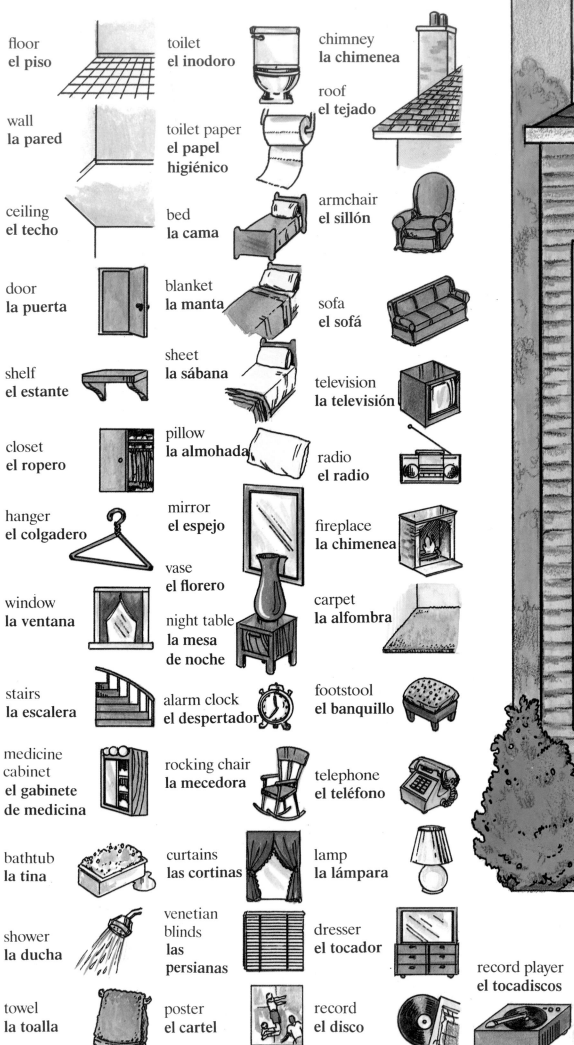

floor
el piso

wall
la pared

ceiling
el techo

door
la puerta

shelf
el estante

closet
el ropero

hanger
el colgadero

window
la ventana

stairs
la escalera

medicine
cabinet
**el gabinete
de medicina**

bathtub
la tina

shower
la ducha

towel
la toalla

toilet
el inodoro

toilet paper
**el papel
higiénico**

bed
la cama

blanket
la manta

sheet
la sábana

pillow
la almohada

mirror
el espejo

vase
el florero

night table
**la mesa
de noche**

alarm clock
el despertador

rocking chair
la mecedora

curtains
las cortinas

venetian
blinds
**las
persianas**

poster
el cartel

chimney
la chimenea

roof
el tejado

armchair
el sillón

sofa
el sofá

television
la televisión

radio
el radio

fireplace
la chimenea

carpet
la alfombra

footstool
el banquillo

telephone
el teléfono

lamp
la lámpara

dresser
el tocador

record
el disco

compact disc
**el disco
compacto**

record player
el tocadiscos

videocassette player
el pasador de videos

bathroom
**el cuarto
de baño**

bedroom
el dormitorio

living room
la sala

dining room
el comedor

kitchen
la cocina

cassette tape
el casete

cassette player
la grabadora

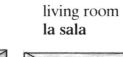

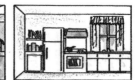

3. The Kitchen
La cocina

counter
el mostrador

oven
el horno

faucet
el grifo

pan
la sartén

paper towels
las toallas de papel

chair
la silla

table
la mesa

refrigerator
la nevera

dishwasher
el lavaplatos

electric mixer
la batidora eléctrica

ice cubes
los cubos de hielo

apron
el delantal

microwave oven
el horno de microondas

freezer
el congelador

food processor
el procesador de alimentos

drawer
el cajón

spatula
la espátula

flour
la harina

stove
la estufa

sink
el fregadero

kettle
la tetera

toaster
el tostador

dishes
los platos

sponge
la esponja

The Utility Room
El cuarto de auxilio

washing machine
la lavadora

iron
la plancha

screw
el tornillo

toolbox
**la caja
de herramientas**

laundry detergent
el detergente

laundry
la ropa sucia

broom
la escoba

mop
el trapeador

screwdriver
el destornillador

wrench
la llave de tuercas

wood
la madera

board
la tabla

vacuum cleaner
la aspiradora

dustpan
la pala de basura

drill
el taladro

electrical outlet
el enchufe

sandpaper
el papel de lija

flashlight
la linterna eléctrica

ironing board
**la mesa
de planchar**

hammer
el martillo

brick
el ladrillo

clothes dryer
la secadora

nail
el clavo

file
la lima

tape measure
la cinta para medir

saw
la sierra

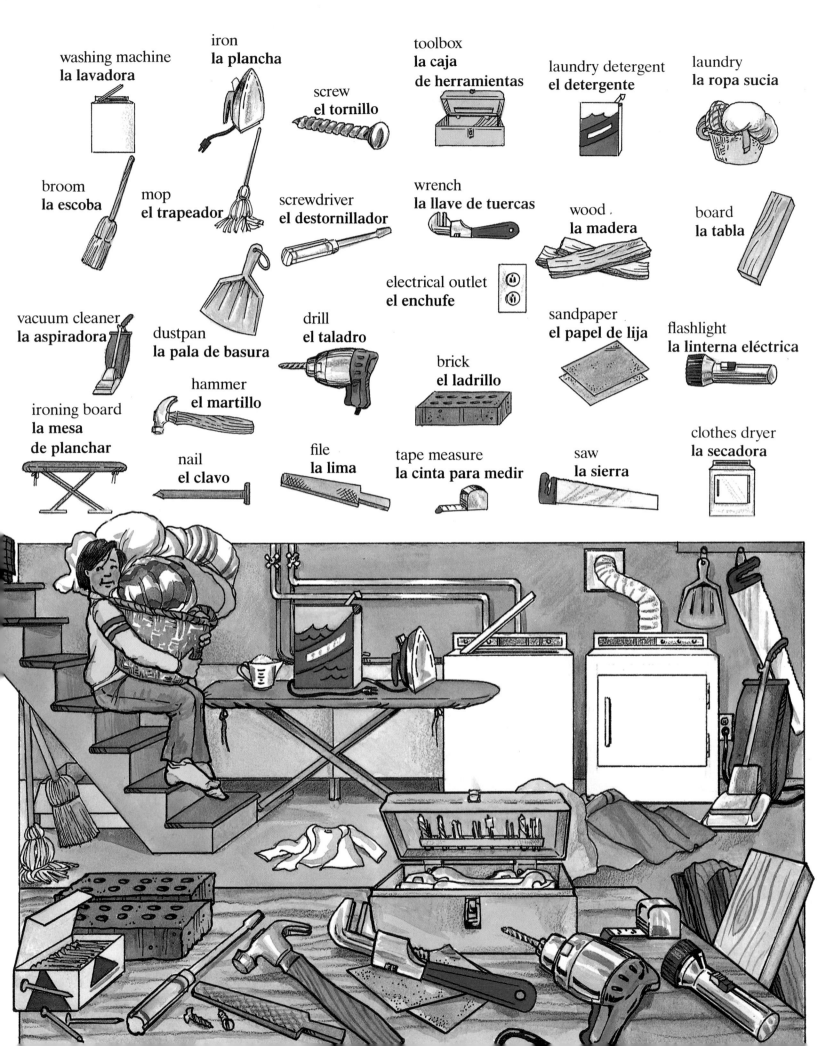

4. The Attic
El desván

trunk
el baúl

box
la caja

dust
el polvo

string
la cuerda

cobweb
la telaraña

ball gown
el vestido de baile

top hat
el sombrero de copa

tuxedo
el esmoquin

hat
el sombrero

feather
la pluma

cowboy hat
el sombrero de vaquero

uniform
el uniforme

cowboy boots
las botas de vaquero

photo album
el álbum de fotos

game
el juego

doll
la muñeca

jigsaw puzzle
el rompecabezas

jump rope
la cuerda de brincar

teddy bear
el osito

toys
los juguetes

whistle
el pito

cards
los naipes

dice
los dados

blocks
los cubos

electric train
el tren eléctrico

magnet
el imán

cradle
la cuna

coloring book
el libro de colorear

music box
la cajita de música

yarn
el hilado

knitting needles
las agujas de tejer

dollhouse
la casa de muñecas

comic books
los libros de cómicos

lightbulb
la bombilla

toy soldiers
los soldados de juguete

movie projector
el proyector de película

umbrella
el paraguas

puppet
el títere

fan
el abanico

marbles
las canicas

rocking horse
el caballo mecedor

chess
el ajedrez

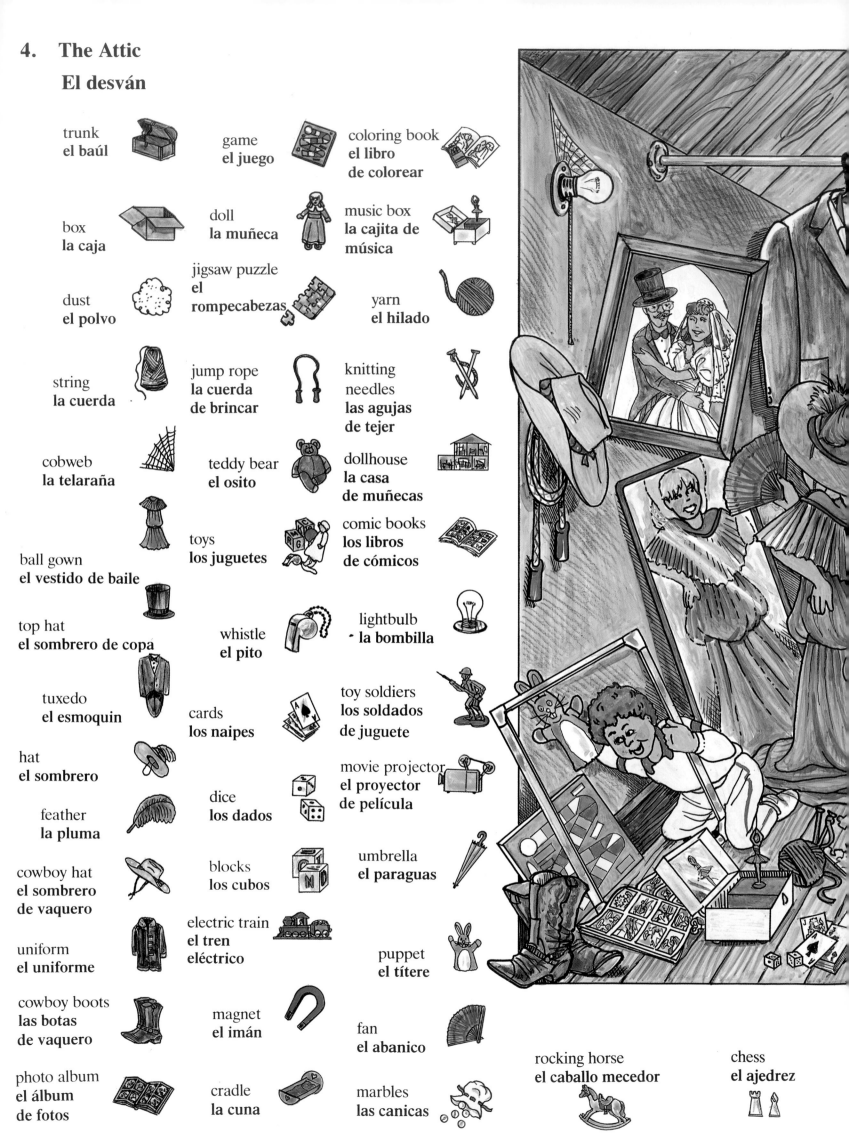

photograph
la fotografía

spinning wheel
el torno de hilar

picture frame
el marco

rocking chair
la mecedora

checkers
el juego de damas

5. The Four Seasons (Weather)
Las cuatro estaciones (El tiempo)

Winter
el invierno

snow
la nieve

ice
el hielo

snowflake
**el copo
de nieve**

icicle
el carámbano

shovel
la pala

snowstorm
**la tormenta
de nieve**

sled
el trineo

snowplow
**la máquina
barredora
de nieve**

snowmobile
**el carro
de nieve**

snowman
**la figura
de nieve**

snowball
**la bola
de nieve**

log
el tronco

**Spring
la primavera**

rain
la lluvia

rainbow
el arco iris

stem
el tallo

bird
el pájaro

worm
el gusano

raindrop
**la gota
de lluvia**

flowers
las flores

flowerbed
**el cuadro
de jardín**

petal
el pétalo

vegetable
garden
**la
hortaliza**

lightning
el relámpago

Summer
el verano

butterfly
la mariposa

fly
la mosca

fly swatter
el matamoscas

fan
el ventilador

sprinkler
la regadera

grasshopper
el saltamontes

lawn mower
la cortadora de grama

barbecue
la barbacoa

hammock
la hamaca

yard
el patio

deck
el patio

garden hose
la manguera de jardín

matches
los fósforos

Fall
el otoño

wind
el viento

leaf
la hoja

branch
la rama

fog
la niebla

rake
el rastrillo

clouds
las nubes

kite
la cometa

puddle
el charco

mud
el lodo

bird's nest
el nido de pájaro

bush
el arbusto

6. At the Supermarket En el supermercado

vegetables
las legumbres

cabbage
la col

lettuce
la lechuga

green beans
**las judías
verdes**

peas
los guisantes

carrots
las zanahorias

tomatoes
los tomates

potatoes
las papas

onions
las cebollas

spinach
las espinacas

avocado
el aguacate

nuts
las nueces

chocolate
el chocolate

candy
los dulces

pie
la empanada

fruit
la fruta

apple
la manzana

orange
la naranja

lemon
el limón

lime
**el limón
verde**

cherries
las cerezas

banana
el plátano

grapes
las uvas

strawberries
las fresas

peach
el durazno

grapefruit
**la
toronja**

melon
el melón

watermelon
la sandía

raspberries
**las
frambuesas**

pineapple
la piña

meat
la carne

eggs
los huevos

butter
la mantequilla

bread
el pan

cheese
el queso

food
la comida

milk
la leche

cookies
**las galletas
dulces**

crackers
las galletas

potato chips
**las papas
fritas a la
inglesa**

bottle
la botella

fruit juice
el jugo

cereal
el cereal

can
la lata

frozen dinner
la cena congelada

soap
el jabón

money
el dinero

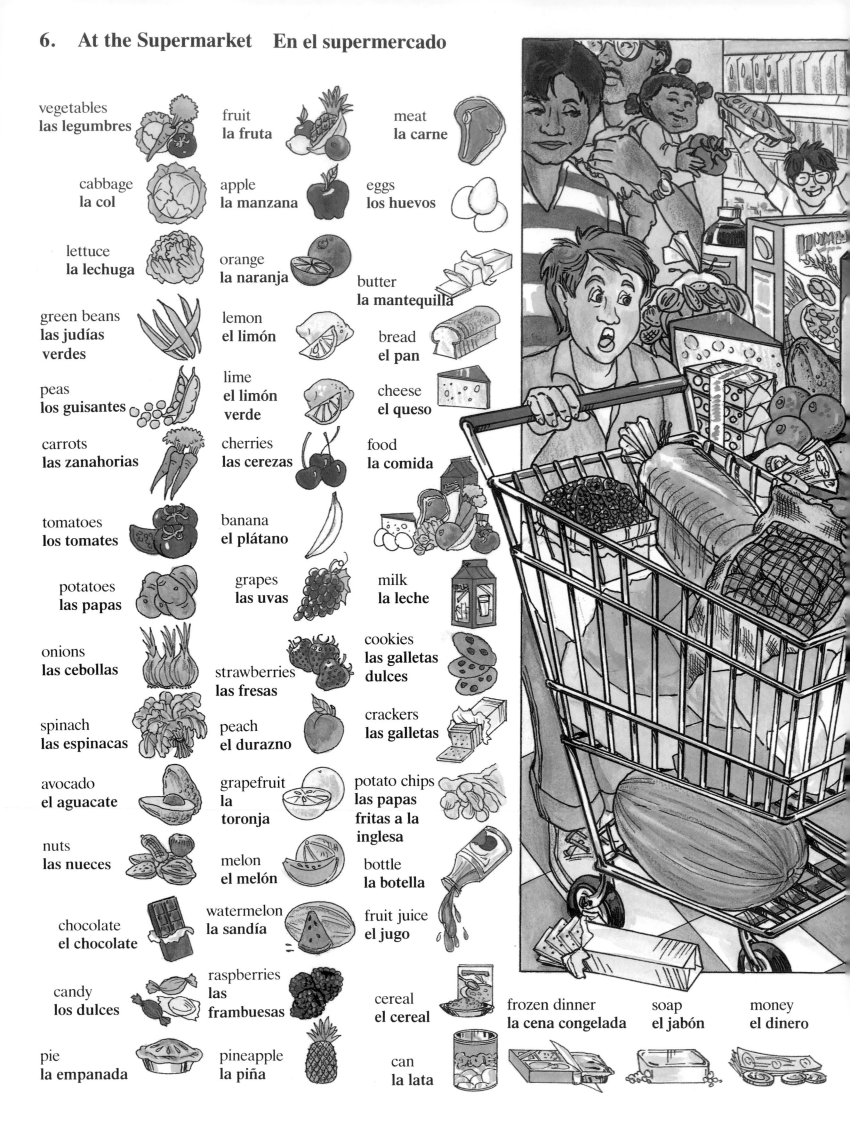

shopping cart
el carrito de compras

shopping
bag
**la bolsa
de compras**

sign
el letrero

scale
la báscula

price
el precio

cash register
la caja

cashier
la cajera

glasses
los anteojos

buckle
la hebilla

belt
el cinturón

pants
los pantalones

collar
el cuello

blouse
la blusa

bracelet
la pulsera

ring
la sortija

skirt
la falda

socks
los calcetines

shoes
los zapatos

underwear
la ropa interior

tie
la corbata

sleeve
la manga

suit
el traje

necklace
el collar

dress
el vestido

bathing suit
el traje de baño

shirt
la camisa

earmuffs
las orejeras

gloves
los guantes

button
el botón

coat
el abrigo

handkerchief
el pañuelo

sweater
el suéter

gym shoes
los zapatos de tenis

shoelace
el cordón

tights
el traje de malla

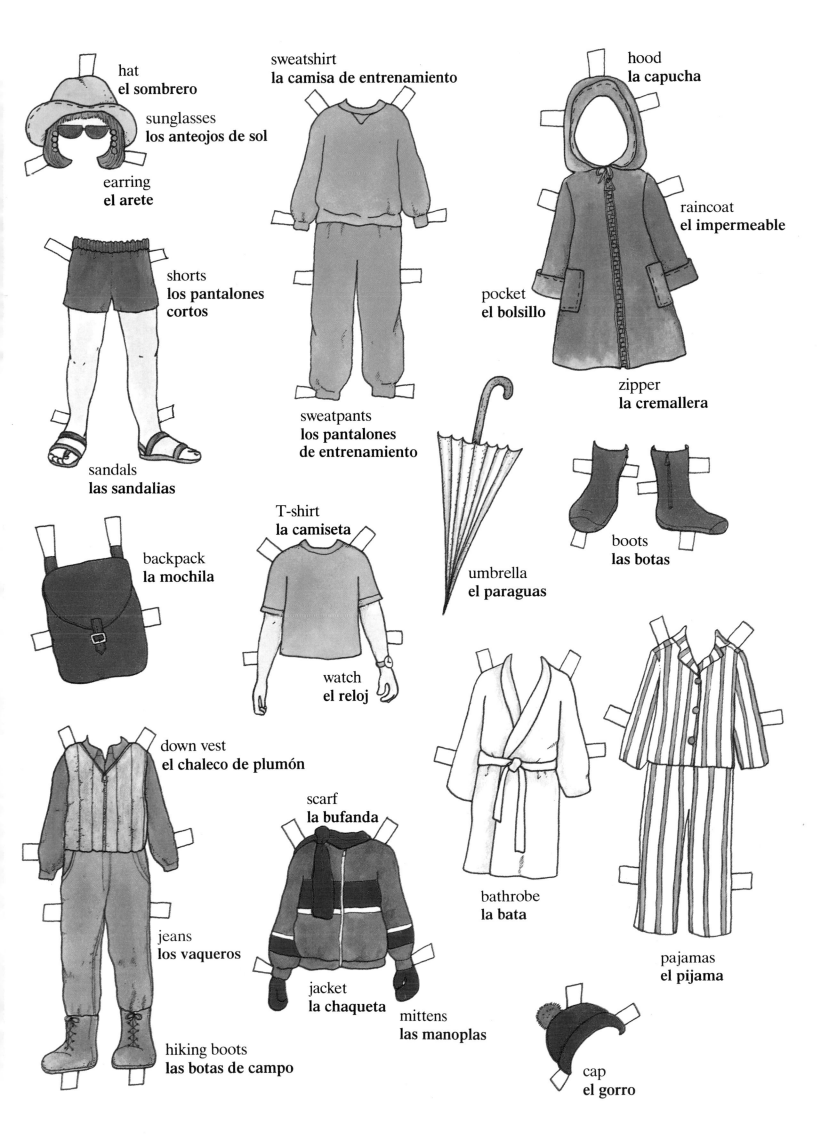

hat
el sombrero

sunglasses
los anteojos de sol

earring
el arete

sweatshirt
la camisa de entrenamiento

hood
la capucha

shorts
los pantalones cortos

raincoat
el impermeable

pocket
el bolsillo

sweatpants
los pantalones de entrenamiento

zipper
la cremallera

sandals
las sandalias

T-shirt
la camiseta

boots
las botas

backpack
la mochila

watch
el reloj

umbrella
el paraguas

down vest
el chaleco de plumón

scarf
la bufanda

bathrobe
la bata

jeans
los vaqueros

pajamas
el pijama

jacket
la chaqueta

mittens
las manoplas

hiking boots
las botas de campo

cap
el gorro

8. In the City En la ciudad

building
el edificio

apartment
building
**el edificio de
apartamentos**

train station
**la estación
del tren**

skyscraper
el rascacielos

fire escape
**la escalera
de incendios**

church
la iglesia

factory
la fábrica

balcony
el balcón

school
la escuela

smokestack
la chimenea

fire station
**la estación
de bomberos**

museum
el museo

traffic lights
el semáforo

police station
**la estación
de policía**

hospital
el hospital

manhole cover
**la tapa
de registro**

jail
la cárcel

drugstore
(pharmacy)
la farmacia

driveway
el camino particular

bookstore
la librería

movie
theater
el cine

parking
lot
el aparcamiento

toy store
**la
juguetería**

restaurant
**el
restaurante**

parking
meter
el parquímetro

grocery store
**la tienda de
comestibles**

clothing
store
el almacén

corner
la esquina

bakery
**la
pastelería**

fire hydrant
**la boca de
incendios**

butcher shop
la carnicería

hotel
el hotel

square
la plaza

fountain
la fuente

traffic jam
**el
embotellamiento
de tráfico**

statue
la estatua

newspaper
**el
periódico**

crane
la grúa

bench
el banco

sign
el letrero

playground
**el patio
de recreo**

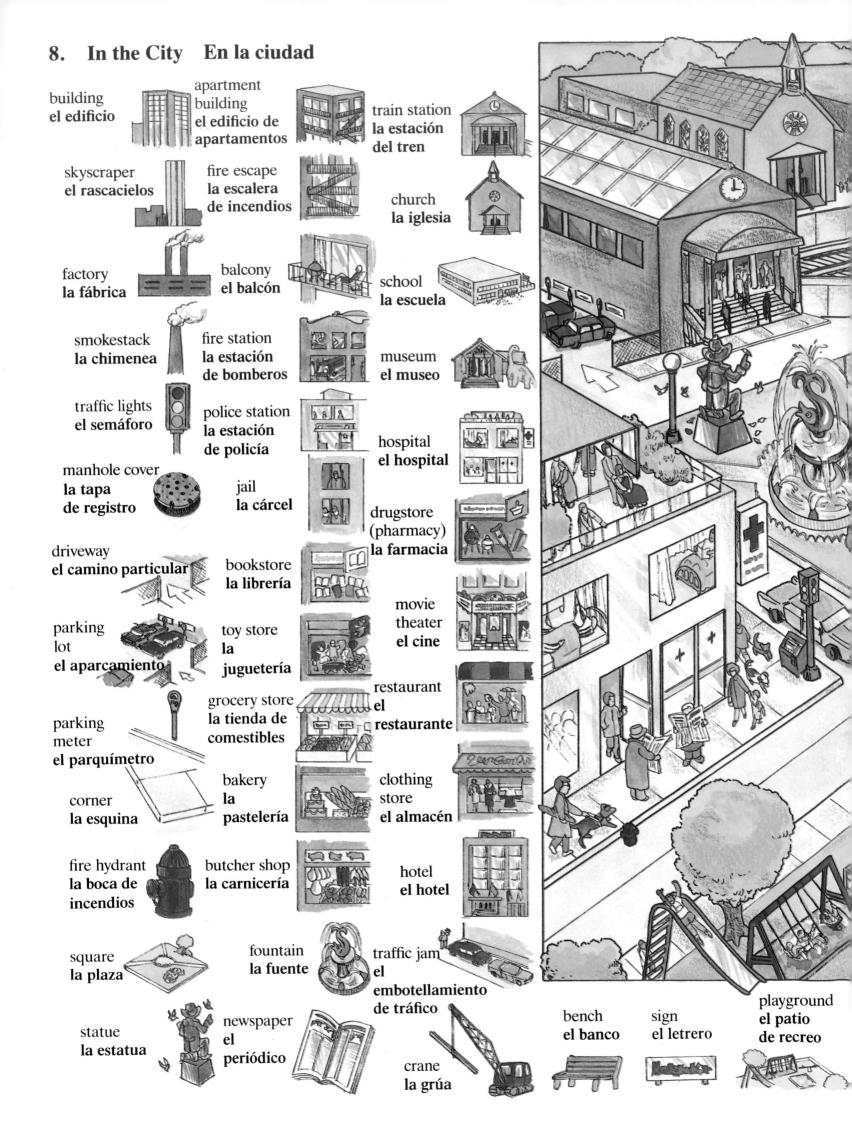

| park
el parque | jungle gym
las barras | swings
los columpios | seesaw
el sube y baja | slide
el tobogán | sandbox
el cajón de arena | beach
la playa |

9. In the Country En el campo

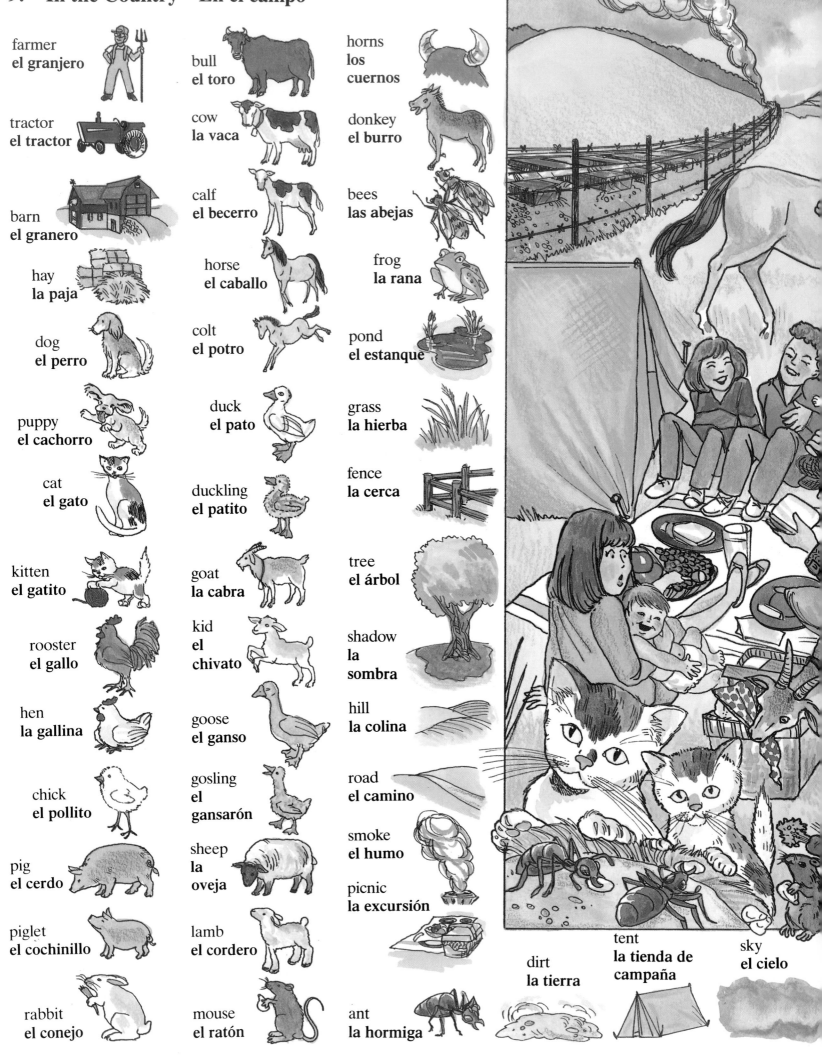

farmer
el granjero

tractor
el tractor

barn
el granero

hay
la paja

dog
el perro

puppy
el cachorro

cat
el gato

kitten
el gatito

rooster
el gallo

hen
la gallina

chick
el pollito

pig
el cerdo

piglet
el cochinillo

rabbit
el conejo

bull
el toro

cow
la vaca

calf
el becerro

horse
el caballo

colt
el potro

duck
el pato

duckling
el patito

goat
la cabra

kid
el chivato

goose
el ganso

gosling
el gansarón

sheep
la oveja

lamb
el cordero

mouse
el ratón

horns
los cuernos

donkey
el burro

bees
las abejas

frog
la rana

pond
el estanque

grass
la hierba

fence
la cerca

tree
el árbol

shadow
la sombra

hill
la colina

road
el camino

smoke
el humo

picnic
la excursión

ant
la hormiga

dirt
la tierra

tent
la tienda de campaña

sky
el cielo

train tracks
las vías de ferrocarril

sleeping bag
el saco de dormir

man
el hombre

woman
la mujer

boy
el niño

girl
la niña

baby
el bebé

farm
la granja

10. In a Restaurant   En un restaurante

breakfast
el desayuno

lunch
el almuerzo

dinner
la cena

yolk
la yema

hamburger
la hamburguesa

steak
el bistec

omelet
la tortilla

sandwich
el bocadillo

fish
el pescado

toast
la tostada

french fries
las papas fritas

ham
el jamón

jam
la mermelada

soup
la sopa

chicken
el pollo

sausages
las salchichas

noodles
los fideos

broccoli
el bróculi

coffee
el café

ketchup
la salsa de tomate

celery
el apio

tea
el té

mustard
la mostaza

salad
la ensalada

cream
la crema

salt
la sal

rice
el arroz

sugar
el azúcar

pepper
la pimienta

mushroom
el hongo

meals
las comidas

ice cream
el helado

tray
la bandeja

candle
la vela

tablecloth
el mantel

waiter
el camarero

cake
la tarta

straw
la paja

waitress
la camarera

gift
el regalo

birthday party
la fiesta de cumpleaños

soft drink
el refresco

knife
el cuchillo

fork
el tenedor

spoon
la cuchara

plate	saucer	cup	glass	bowl	napkin	menu
el plato	el platillo	la taza	el vaso	el tazón	la servilleta	el menú

11. The Doctor's Office   La oficina del médico

doctor
la médica

nurse
el enfermero

patient
el paciente

medicine
la medicina

pill
la pastilla

thermometer
el termómetro

bandage
la venda
adhesiva

cast
la escayola

sling
el cabestrillo

hypodermic needle
la aguja
hipodérmica

blood
la sangre

cane
el bastón

crutch
la muleta

stethoscope
el estetoscopio

examining table
la camilla

sneeze
el estornudo

arm
el brazo

elbow
el codo

hand
la mano

finger
el dedo

thumb
el pulgar

leg
la pierna

wheelchair
la silla
de ruedas

foot
el pie

ankle
el tobillo

toe
el dedo
(del pie)

shoulder
el hombro

back
la espalda

chest
el pecho

knee
la rodilla

The Dentist's Office   La oficina del dentista

dentist
el dentista

waiting room
**la sala
de espera**

eyebrow
la ceja

braces
los frenos

dental hygienist
la higienista dental

magazines
las revistas

eyes
los ojos

head
la cabeza

tooth
el diente

X ray
los rayos X

nose
la nariz

face
la cara

toothbrush
**el cepillo
de dientes**

smile
la sonrisa

mouth
la boca

cheek
la mejilla

toothpaste
**la pasta
dentífrica**

lips
los labios

chin
la barbilla

dental floss
la seda dental

tongue
la lengua

ear
la oreja

forehead
la frente

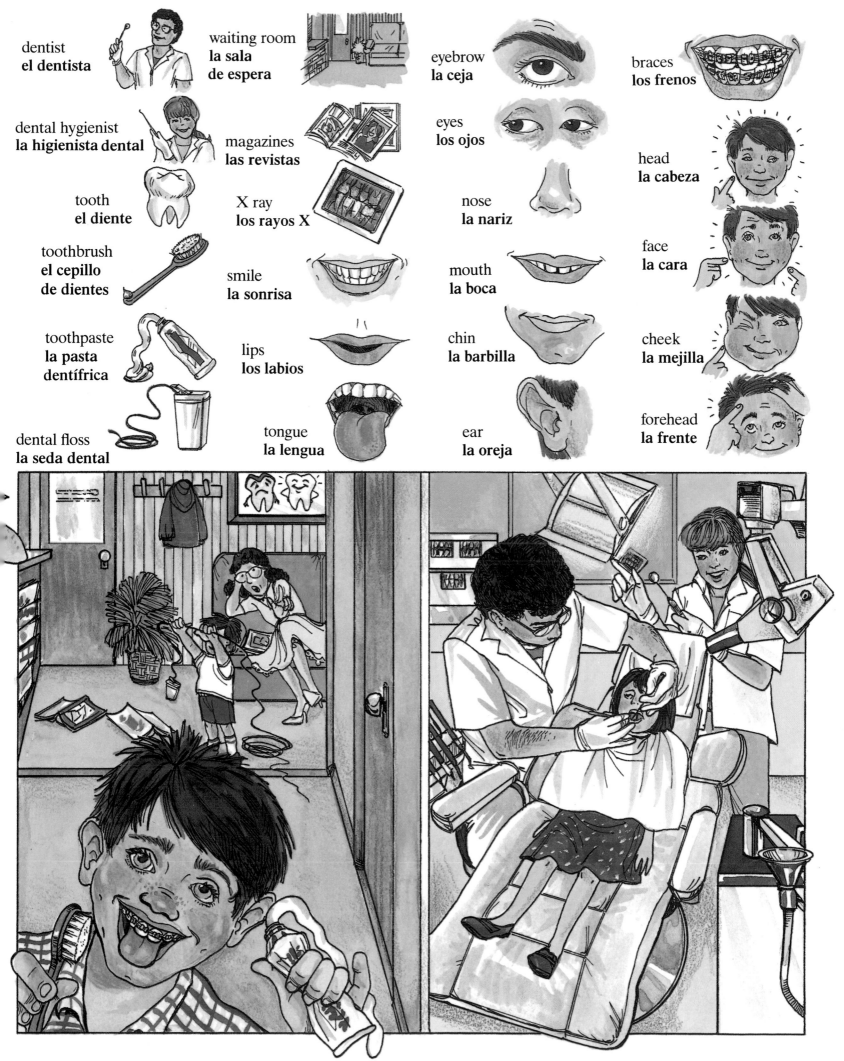

12. The Barber Shop/Beauty Salon
La peluquería de caballeros y señoras

hairstylist
la peluquera

shampoo
el champú

suds
la espuma

comb
el peine

brush
el cepillo

scissors
las tijeras

curlers
los rollos

curling iron
el rizador

barber
el barbero

shaving cream
la crema de afeitar

razor
la navaja de afeitar

beard
la barba

mousse
la espuma de pelo

manicurist
la manicura

fingernail
la uña

nail polish
el esmalte

lipstick
el lápiz de labios

mascara
el rimel

powder
el polvo

hair dryer
el secador

bald
calvo

mustache
el bigote

freckles
las pecas

pedicurist
la pedicura

barrette
el pasador

braid
la trenza

wavy
ondulado

straight
liso

curly
rizado

short
corto

long
largo

black
negro

brown
castaño

blond
rubio

red
pelirrojo

toenail
la uña (del pie)

nail clippers
el cortaúñas

nail file
la lima

crew cut
el corte a cepillo

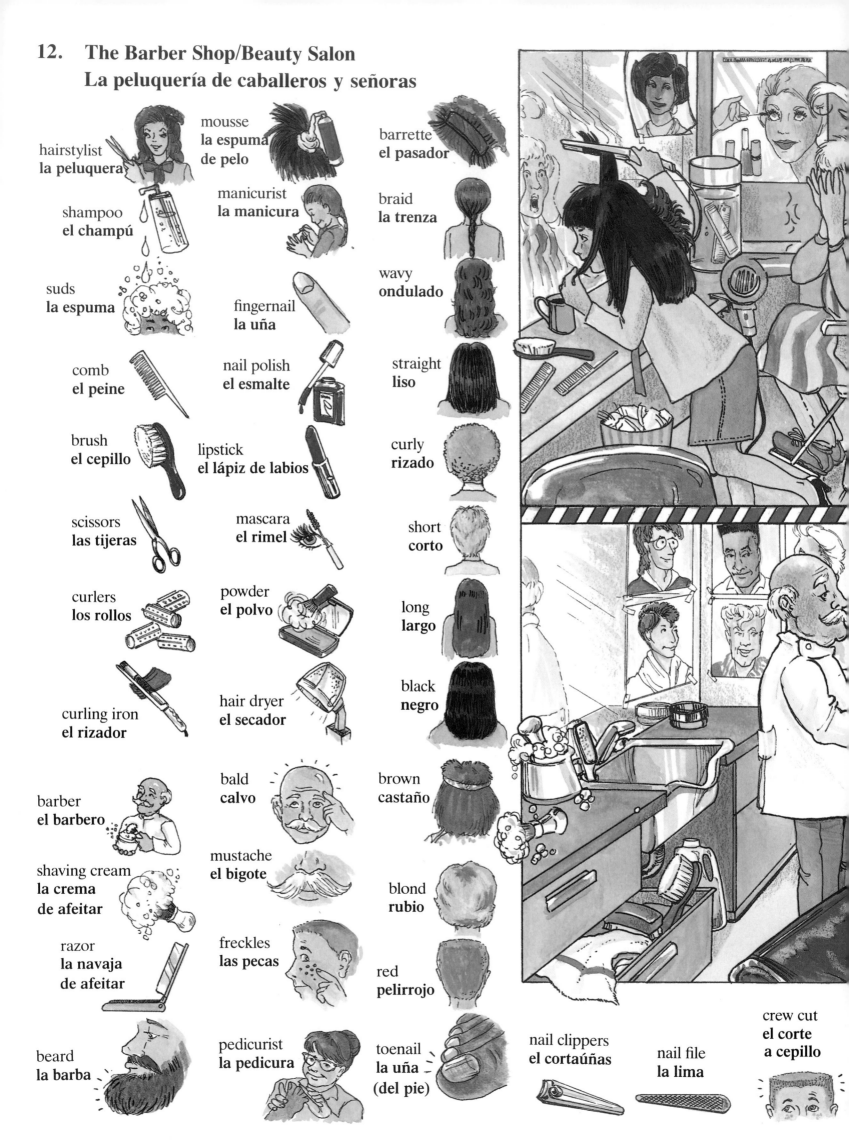

ponytail
la cola de caballo

bangs
el flequillo

bun
el moño

part
la raya

hair spray
la laca

hair
el pelo

blow dryer
el secador

13. The Post Office El correo

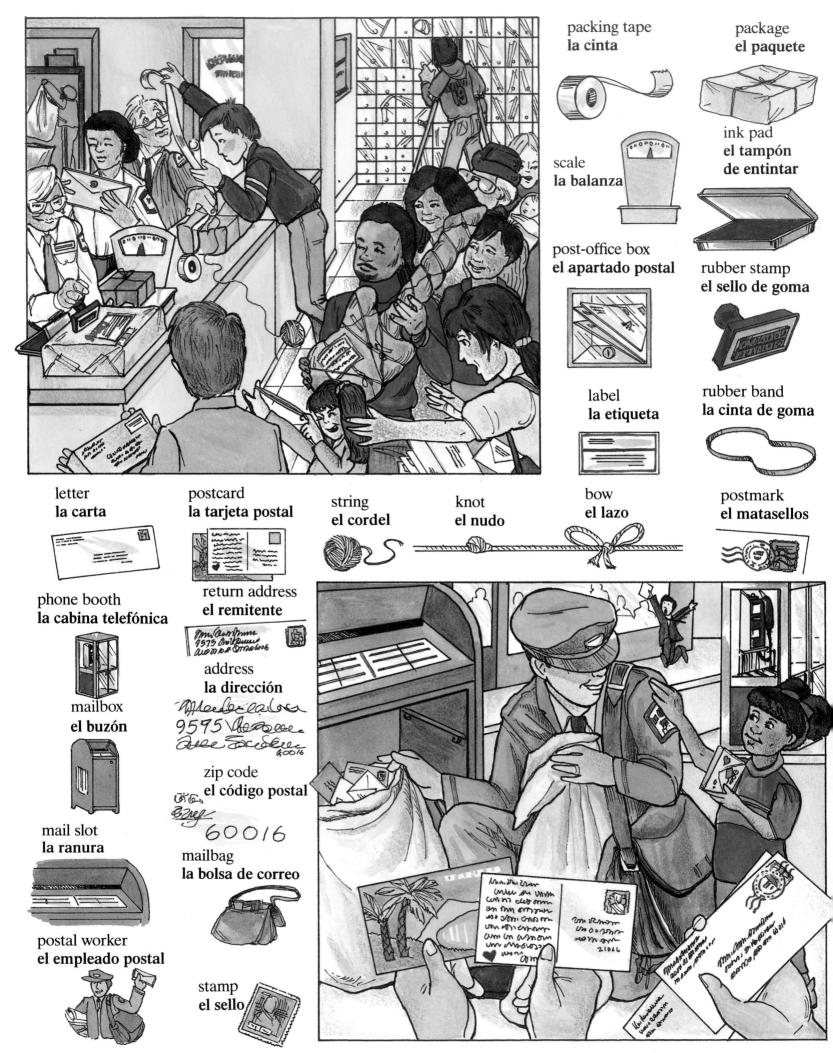

packing tape
la cinta

package
el paquete

scale
la balanza

ink pad
el tampón
de entintar

post-office box
el apartado postal

rubber stamp
el sello de goma

label
la etiqueta

rubber band
la cinta de goma

letter
la carta

postcard
la tarjeta postal

string
el cordel

knot
el nudo

bow
el lazo

postmark
el matasellos

phone booth
la cabina telefónica

return address
el remitente

address
la dirección

9595

60016

zip code
el código postal

60016

mailbox
el buzón

mail slot
la ranura

mailbag
la bolsa de correo

postal worker
el empleado postal

stamp
el sello

The Bank   El banco

paper clip
el sujetapapeles

security guard
**el guardia
de seguridad**

security camera
**la cámara
de seguridad**

safe
la caja fuerte

credit card
**la tarjeta
de crédito**

typewriter
**la máquina
de escribir**

safety deposit box
la caja de seguridad

notepad
el cuaderno

teller
la cajera

wallet
la billetera

key
la llave

lock
la cerradura

file cabinet
el archivo

receptionist
la recepcionista

bill
el billete

coin
la moneda

check
el cheque

checkbook
**el talonario
de cheques**

piggy bank
la hucha

signature
la firma

drive-in
**el servicio
para automovilistas**

automatic teller
**el cajero
automático**

14. At the Gas Station   En la gasolinera

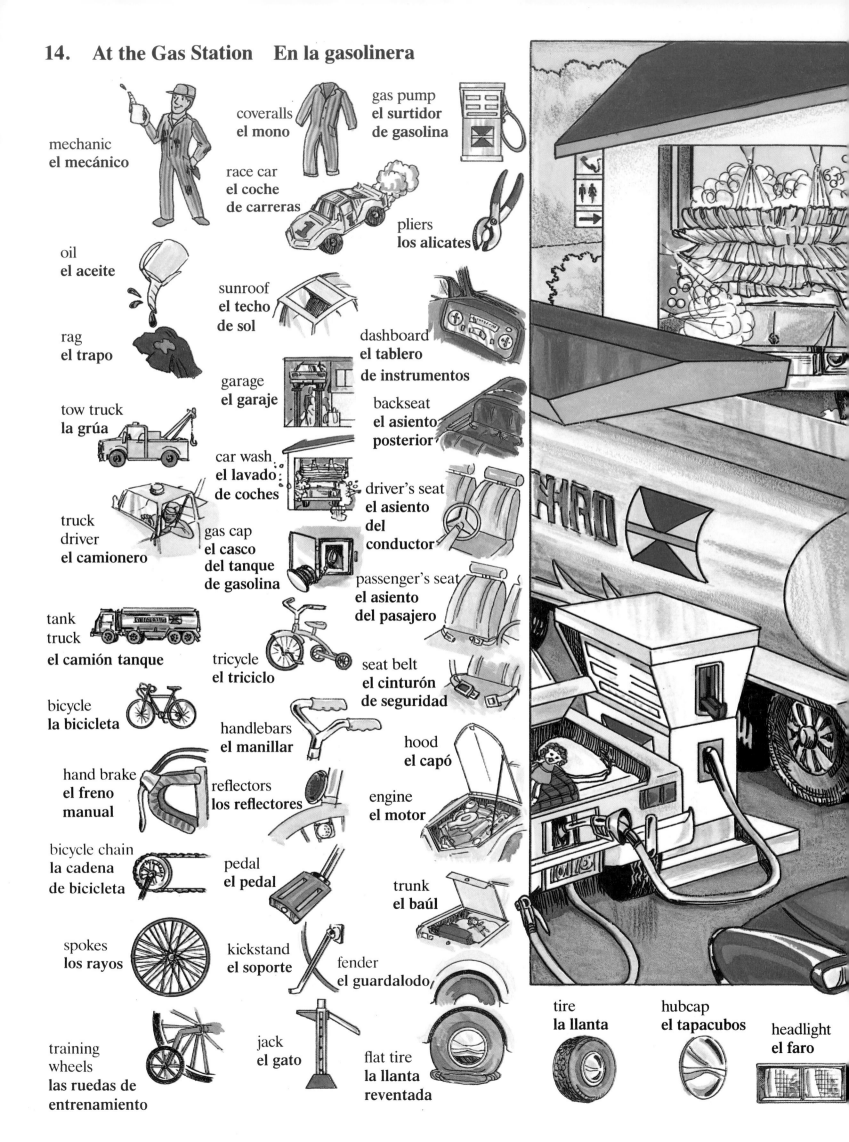

mechanic
el mecánico

coveralls
el mono

gas pump
**el surtidor
de gasolina**

race car
**el coche
de carreras**

pliers
los alicates

oil
el aceite

sunroof
**el techo
de sol**

dashboard
**el tablero
de instrumentos**

rag
el trapo

garage
el garaje

backseat
**el asiento
posterior**

tow truck
la grúa

car wash
**el lavado
de coches**

driver's seat
**el asiento
del
conductor**

truck
driver
el camionero

gas cap
**el casco
del tanque
de gasolina**

passenger's seat
**el asiento
del pasajero**

tank
truck
el camión tanque

tricycle
el triciclo

seat belt
**el cinturón
de seguridad**

bicycle
la bicicleta

handlebars
el manillar

hood
el capó

hand brake
**el freno
manual**

reflectors
los reflectores

engine
el motor

bicycle chain
**la cadena
de bicicleta**

pedal
el pedal

trunk
el baúl

spokes
los rayos

kickstand
el soporte

fender
el guardalodo

training
wheels
**las ruedas de
entrenamiento**

jack
el gato

flat tire
**la llanta
reventada**

tire
la llanta

hubcap
el tapacubos

headlight
el faro

| brake lights
**los faros
de freno** | windshield
el parabrisas | windshield wipers
los limpiaparabrisas | steering
wheel
el volante | rearview mirror
el espejo retrovisor | air hose
**la manga
de aire** | door handle
la manilla |

15. People in Our Community Las personas de nuestra comunidad

saleswoman
la vendedora

judge
la juez

cook
el cocinero

model
la modelo

electrician
el electricista

athlete
el atleta

fire fighter
el bombero

architect
la arquitecta

doorman
el portero

bus driver
**la conductora
de autobús**

plumber
el plomero

television repairer
el reparador de televisión

taxi driver
el taxista

fashion designer
la diseñadora de modas

tour guide
la guía

bookseller
el librero

librarian
el bibliotecario

computer programmer
la programadora de computadoras

photographer
el fotógrafo

gardener
el jardinero

painter
el pintor

salesman
el vendedor

secretary
la secretaria

weather forecaster
el meteorólogo

16. Going Places (Transportation) El transporte

car
el coche

airplane
el avión

jeep
el jeep

hang glider
el planeador

hot-air balloon
el globo

van
la camioneta

sail
la vela

helicopter
el helicóptero

scooter
el patinete

sailboat
el barco de vela

rowboat
el bote de remos

skateboard
el monopatín

tugboat
el barco remolcador

cruise ship
el crucero

roller skates
los patines de ruedas

train
el tren

motorboat
la lancha

canoe
la canoa

taxi
el taxi

police car
el coche de policía

blimp
el dirigible

stroller
el cochecito de niño

truck
el camión

camper
la caravana

baby carriage
el cochecito

fire engine
el coche de bomberos

bicycle
la bicicleta

cement mixer
el mezclador de cemento

ambulance
la ambulancia

traffic lights
el semáforo

motorcycle
la motocicleta

Stop!
¡Alto!

bus
el autobús

Wait!
¡Espere!

school bus
el autobús escolar

lighthouse
el faro

Go!
¡Adelante!

street
la calle

intersection
la intersección

sidewalk
la acera

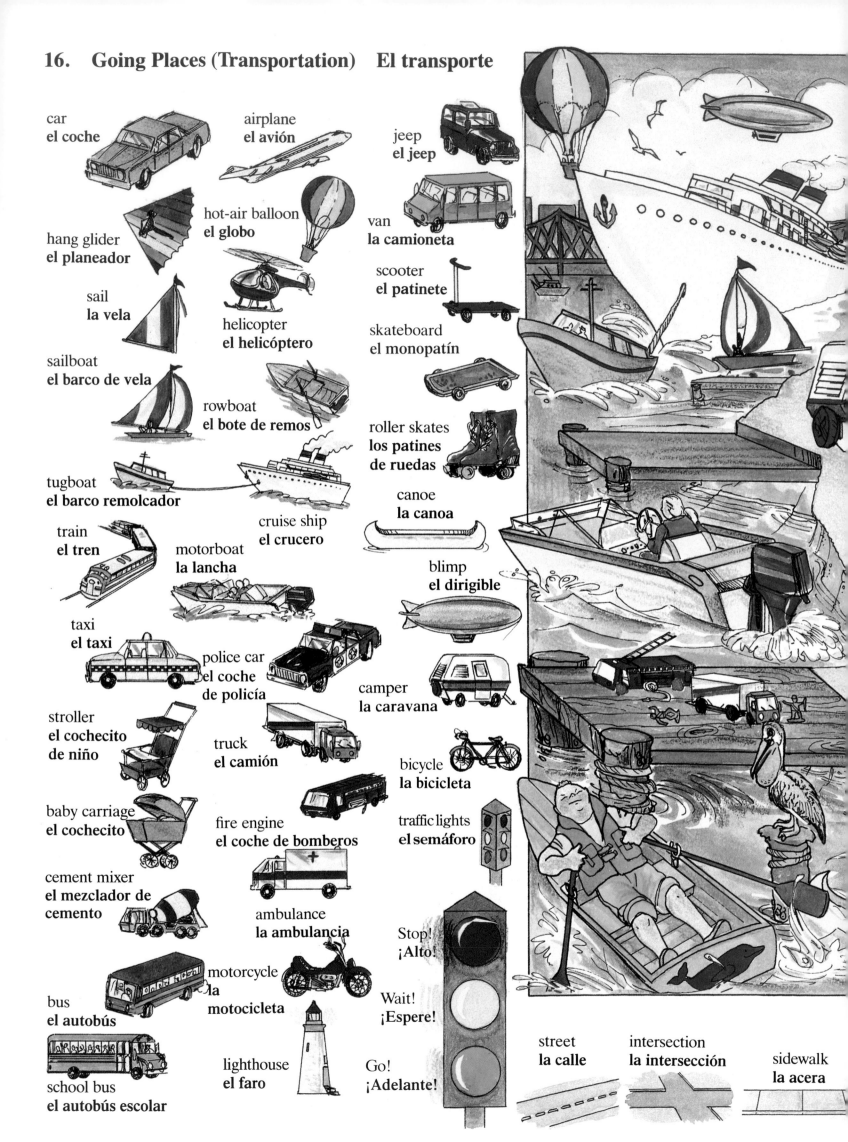

dock
el muelle

bus stop
**la parada
de autobús**

bridge
el puente

crosswalk
**el cruce
de peatones**

oar
el remo

boat
el barco

stop sign
**la señal
de alto**

17. The Airport   El aeropuerto

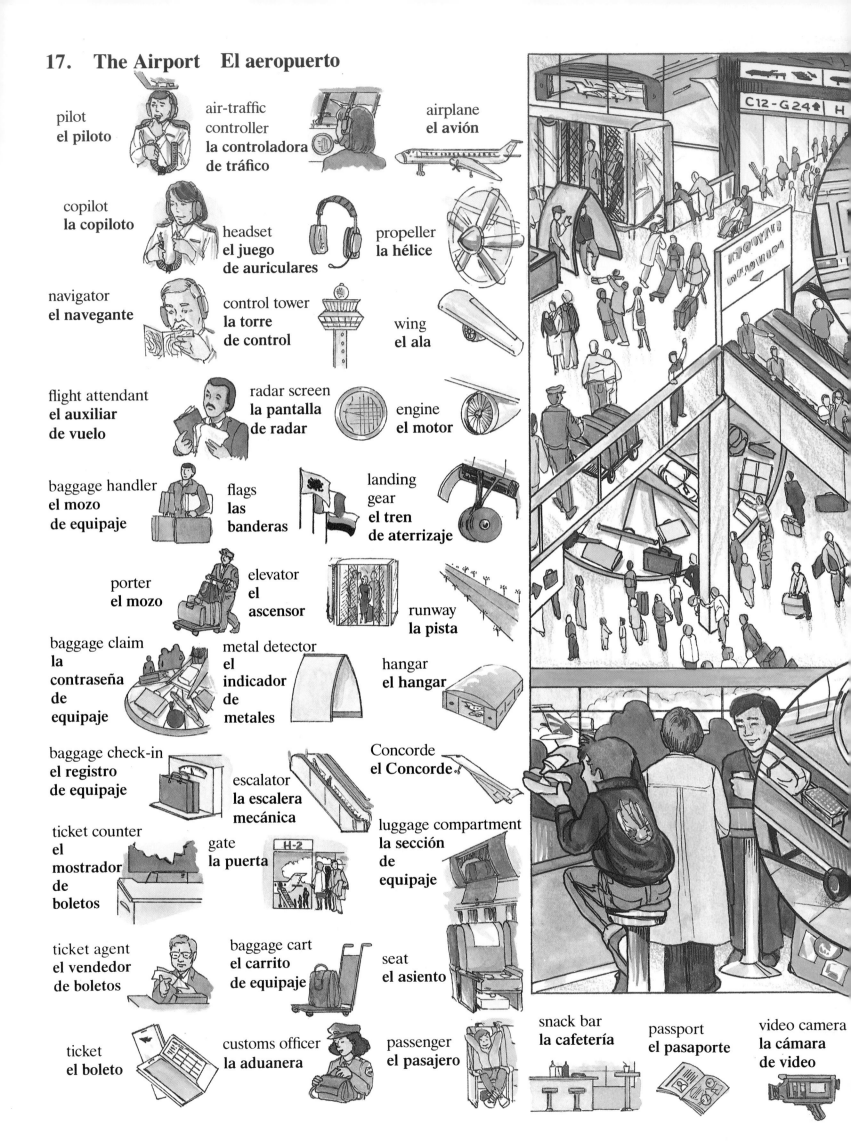

pilot
el piloto

air-traffic
controller
**la controladora
de tráfico**

airplane
el avión

copilot
la copiloto

headset
**el juego
de auriculares**

propeller
la hélice

navigator
el navegante

control tower
**la torre
de control**

wing
el ala

flight attendant
**el auxiliar
de vuelo**

radar screen
**la pantalla
de radar**

engine
el motor

baggage handler
**el mozo
de equipaje**

flags
**las
banderas**

landing
gear
**el tren
de aterrizaje**

porter
el mozo

elevator
**el
ascensor**

runway
la pista

baggage claim
**la
contraseña
de
equipaje**

metal detector
**el
indicador
de
metales**

hangar
el hangar

baggage check-in
**el registro
de equipaje**

escalator
**la escalera
mecánica**

Concorde
el Concorde

ticket counter
**el
mostrador
de
boletos**

gate
la puerta

H-2

luggage compartment
**la sección
de
equipaje**

ticket agent
**el vendedor
de boletos**

baggage cart
**el carrito
de equipaje**

seat
el asiento

ticket
el boleto

customs officer
la aduanera

passenger
el pasajero

snack bar
la cafetería

passport
el pasaporte

video camera
**la cámara
de video**

C12-G24 H

tennis racket
la raqueta de tenis

binoculars
los prismáticos

camera
la cámara

purse
el bolso

suitcase
la maleta

garment bag
la maleta para vestidos y trajes

briefcase
la cartera

18. Sports   Los deportes

gymnastics
la gimnasia

goggles
las gafas protectoras

wrestling
la lucha libre

cross-country skiing
el esquí nórdico

cycling
el ciclismo

soccer
el fútbol

long jump
el salto largo

car racing
las carreras de coches

baseball
la pelota (de béisbol)

boxing
el boxeo

badminton
el badminton

net
la red

football
el fútbol americano

skates
los patines

skating
el patinaje

hurdles
las vallas

golf
el golf

medal
la medalla

horseback riding
la equitación

baseball
el béisbol

jogging
el jogging

hockey
el hockey

tennis
el tenis

diving
el salto al agua

weight lifting
el levantamiento de pesos

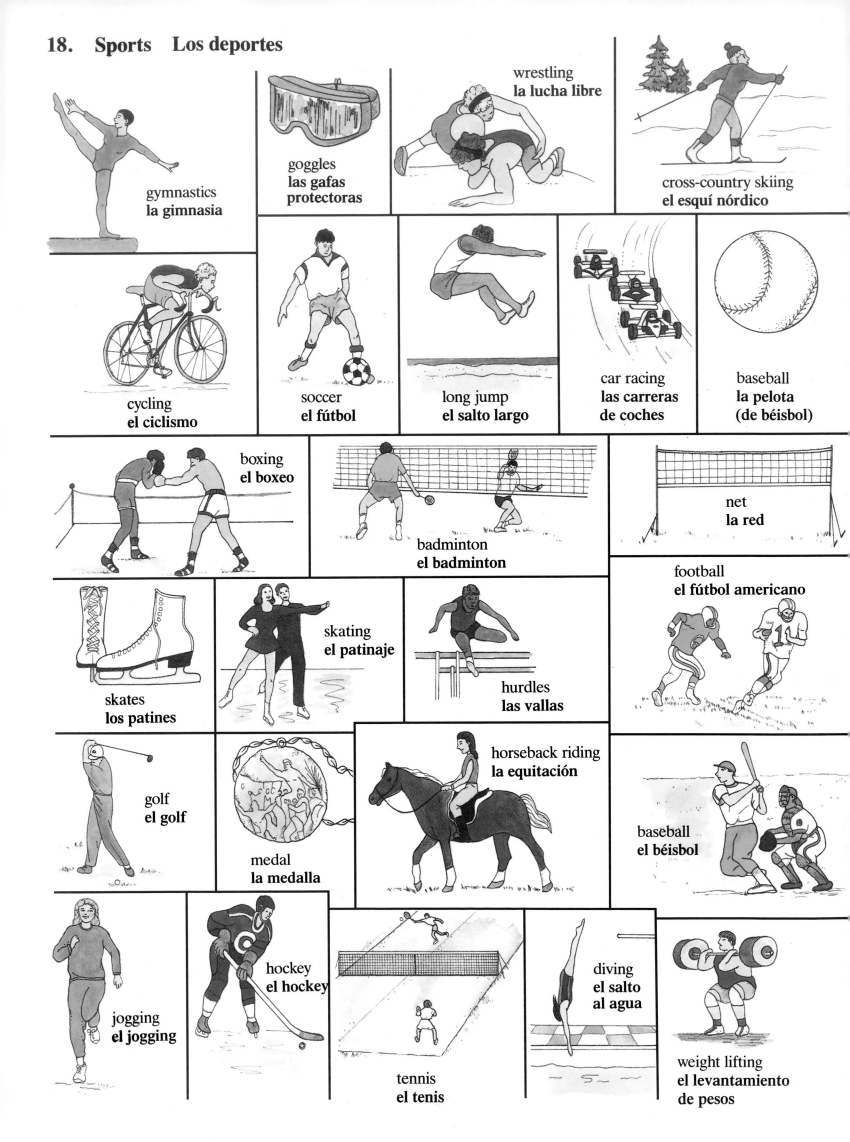

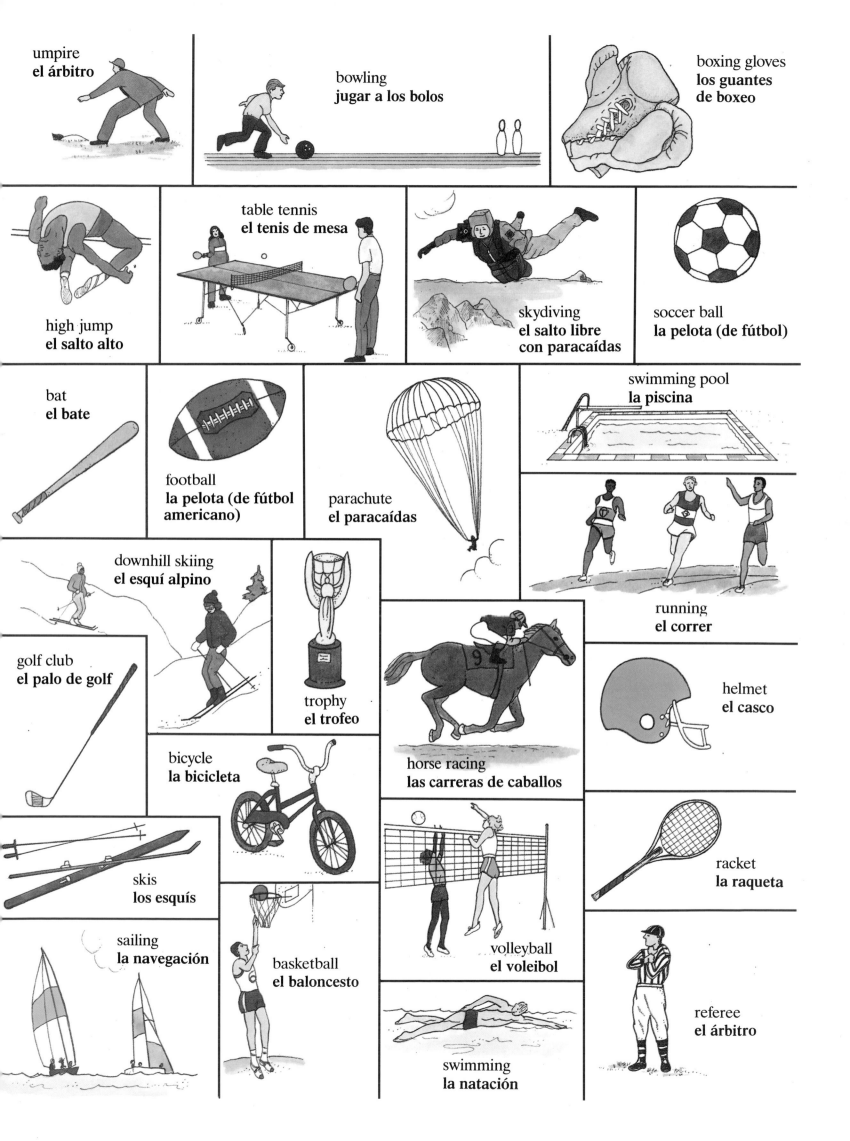

umpire
el árbitro

bowling
jugar a los bolos

boxing gloves
los guantes de boxeo

high jump
el salto alto

table tennis
el tenis de mesa

skydiving
el salto libre con paracaídas

soccer ball
la pelota (de fútbol)

bat
el bate

football
la pelota (de fútbol americano)

parachute
el paracaídas

swimming pool
la piscina

downhill skiing
el esquí alpino

trophy
el trofeo

running
el correr

golf club
el palo de golf

bicycle
la bicicleta

horse racing
las carreras de caballos

helmet
el casco

skis
los esquís

racket
la raqueta

sailing
la navegación

basketball
el baloncesto

volleyball
el voleibol

swimming
la natación

referee
el árbitro

19. The Talent Show   El espectáculo

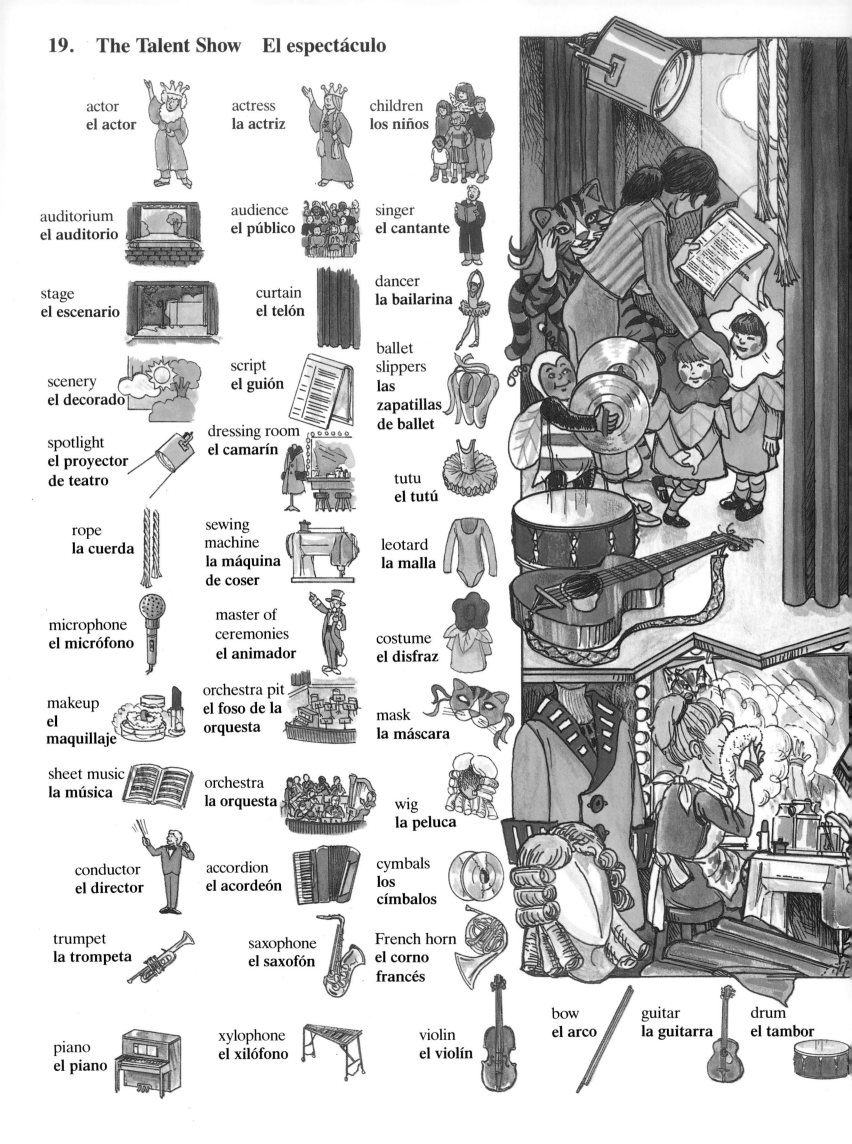

actor
el actor

actress
la actriz

children
los niños

auditorium
el auditorio

audience
el público

singer
el cantante

stage
el escenario

curtain
el telón

dancer
la bailarina

scenery
el decorado

script
el guión

ballet
slippers
**las
zapatillas
de ballet**

spotlight
**el proyector
de teatro**

dressing room
el camarín

tutu
el tutú

rope
la cuerda

sewing
machine
**la máquina
de coser**

leotard
la malla

microphone
el micrófono

master of
ceremonies
el animador

makeup
**el
maquillaje**

orchestra pit
**el foso de la
orquesta**

costume
el disfraz

sheet music
la música

orchestra
la orquesta

mask
la máscara

wig
la peluca

conductor
el director

accordion
el acordeón

cymbals
**los
címbalos**

trumpet
la trompeta

saxophone
el saxofón

French horn
**el corno
francés**

bow
el arco

guitar
la guitarra

drum
el tambor

piano
el piano

xylophone
el xilófono

violin
el violín

tuba
la tuba

flute
la flauta

trombone
el trombón

clarinet
el clarinete

cello
el violoncelo

strings
las cuerdas

harp
el arpa

20. At the Zoo En el jardín zoológico

zookeeper
**el guardián
de zoológico**

elephant
el elefante

animals
los animales

rhinoceros
el rinoceronte

ostrich
el avestruz

fox
el zorro

lion
el león

bear
el oso

wolf
el lobo

tiger
el tigre

bear cub
**el cachorro
de oso**

alligator
el caimán

tiger cub
**el cachorro
de tigre**

polar bear
el oso polar

zebra
la cebra

jaguar
el jaguar

panda
el panda

giraffe
la jirafa

leopard
el leopardo

gorilla
el gorila

monkey
el mono

flamingo
el flamenco

parrot
el loro

hippopotamus
el hipopótamo

owl
la lechuza

snake
la serpiente

kangaroo
el canguro

swan
el cisne

seal
la foca

deer
el ciervo

penguin
el pingüino

walrus
la morsa

lizard
el lagarto

peacock
**el pavo
real**

hump
la giba

turtle
la tortuga

eagle
el águila

camel
el camello

horns
los cuernos

wings
las alas

feathers
las plumas

beak
el pico

paw
la pata

claws
las garras

mane
la melena

tail
la cola

hoof
el casco

stripes
las rayas

spots
las manchas

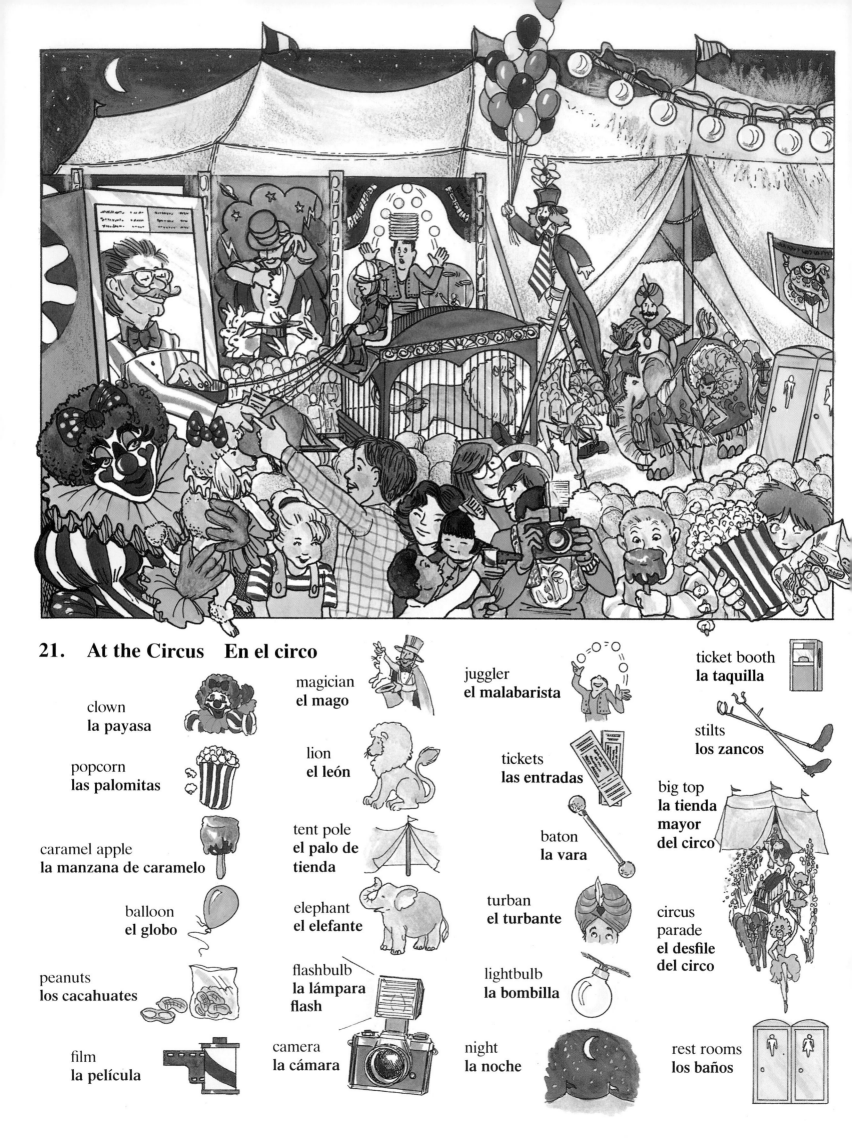

21. At the Circus En el circo

clown
la payasa

magician
el mago

juggler
el malabarista

ticket booth
la taquilla

popcorn
las palomitas

lion
el león

tickets
las entradas

stilts
los zancos

caramel apple
la manzana de caramelo

tent pole
el palo de tienda

baton
la vara

big top
la tienda mayor del circo

balloon
el globo

elephant
el elefante

turban
el turbante

circus parade
el desfile del circo

peanuts
los cacahuates

flashbulb
la lámpara flash

lightbulb
la bombilla

film
la película

camera
la cámara

night
la noche

rest rooms
los baños

bareback rider
la jinete

tightrope walker
la gimnasta de la cuerda floja

trapeze
el trapecio

trapeze artist
el trapecista

tightrope
la cuerda floja

cage
la jaula

band
la banda

lion tamer
el domador de fieras

whip
el látigo

unicycle
el monociclo

safety net
la red de seguridad

ring
la pista de circo

hoop
el aro

rope ladder
la escalera de cuerda

rope
la cuerda

handstand
el farol

acrobat
el acróbata

headstand
la parada de cabeza

somersault
el salto mortal

cartwheel
la voltereta lateral

cotton candy
el algodón de azúcar

cape
la capa

ringmaster
el maestro de ceremonias

22. In the Ocean
En el mar

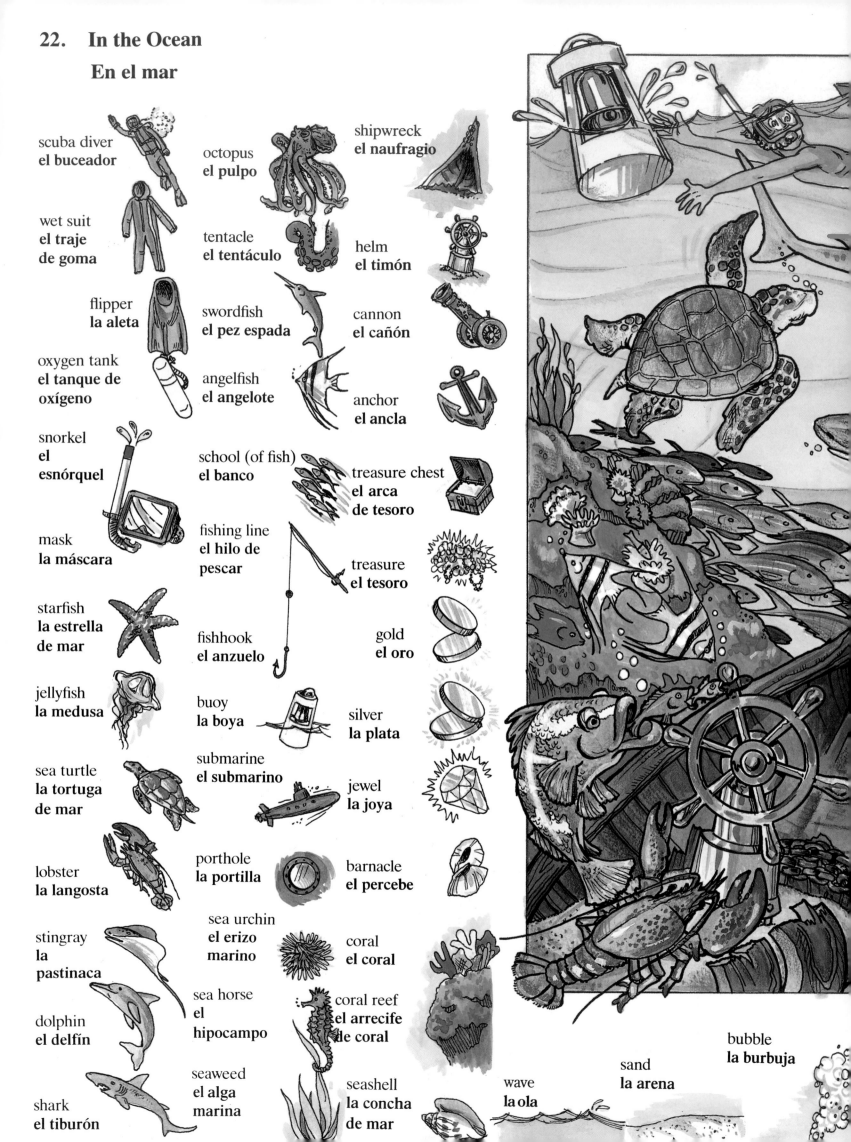

scuba diver
el buceador

wet suit
el traje de goma

flipper
la aleta

oxygen tank
el tanque de oxígeno

snorkel
el esnórquel

mask
la máscara

starfish
la estrella de mar

jellyfish
la medusa

sea turtle
la tortuga de mar

lobster
la langosta

stingray
la pastinaca

dolphin
el delfín

shark
el tiburón

octopus
el pulpo

tentacle
el tentáculo

swordfish
el pez espada

angelfish
el angelote

school (of fish)
el banco

fishing line
el hilo de pescar

fishhook
el anzuelo

buoy
la boya

submarine
el submarino

porthole
la portilla

sea urchin
el erizo marino

sea horse
el hipocampo

seaweed
el alga marina

shipwreck
el naufragio

helm
el timón

cannon
el cañón

anchor
el ancla

treasure chest
el arca de tesoro

treasure
el tesoro

gold
el oro

silver
la plata

jewel
la joya

barnacle
el percebe

coral
el coral

coral reef
el arrecife de coral

seashell
la concha de mar

wave
la ola

sand
la arena

bubble
la burbuja

scales
las escamas

gills
las agallas

fin
la aleta

clam
la almeja

crab
el cangrejo

squid
el calamar

whale
la ballena

23. Space
El espacio

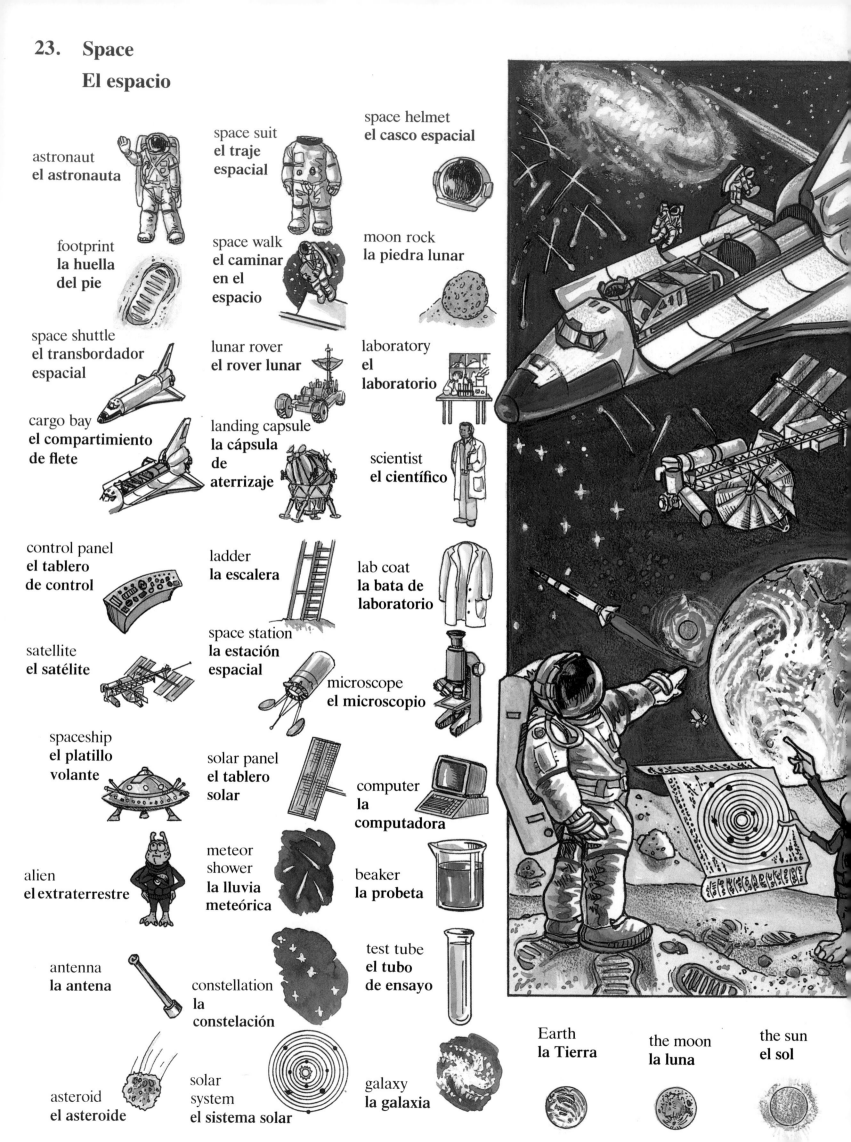

astronaut
el astronauta

footprint
**la huella
del pie**

space shuttle
**el transbordador
espacial**

cargo bay
**el compartimiento
de flete**

control panel
**el tablero
de control**

satellite
el satélite

spaceship
**el platillo
volante**

alien
el extraterrestre

antenna
la antena

asteroid
el asteroide

space suit
**el traje
espacial**

space walk
**el caminar
en el
espacio**

lunar rover
el rover lunar

landing capsule
**la cápsula
de
aterrizaje**

ladder
la escalera

space station
**la estación
espacial**

solar panel
**el tablero
solar**

meteor
shower
**la lluvia
meteórica**

constellation
**la
constelación**

solar
system
el sistema solar

space helmet
el casco espacial

moon rock
la piedra lunar

laboratory
**el
laboratorio**

scientist
el científico

lab coat
**la bata de
laboratorio**

microscope
el microscopio

computer
**la
computadora**

beaker
la probeta

test tube
**el tubo
de ensayo**

galaxy
la galaxia

Earth
la Tierra

the moon
la luna

the sun
el sol

planet
el planeta

rings
los anillos

crater
el cráter

stars
las estrellas

comet
el cometa

nebula
la nebulosa

rocket
el cohete

robot
el robot

24. Human History
La historia de la humanidad

rock
la piedra

boulder
la roca

bone
el hueso

insect
el insecto

fern
el helecho

tree
el árbol

cave
la caverna

fur
la piel

fire
el fuego

stick
el palo

wheel
la rueda

flint
el pedernal

arrowhead
**la punta
de flecha**

club
el garrote

spear
la lanza

mammoth
el mamut

tusk
el colmillo

trunk
la trompa

bison
el bisonte

paint
la pintura

cave drawing
**el dibujo
de caverna**

hut
la cabaña

corn
el maíz

wheat
el trigo

weaver
la tejedora

loom
el telar

kiln
el horno

potter
el alfarero

pot
el pote

clay
el barro

cart
la carreta

basket
la canasta

leather
el cuero

fishing
la pesca

hunter
el cazador

well
el pozo

bucket
el balde

water
el agua

cloth
la tela

saber-toothed tiger
**el tigre de dientes
de sable**

crop
la cosecha

field
el campo

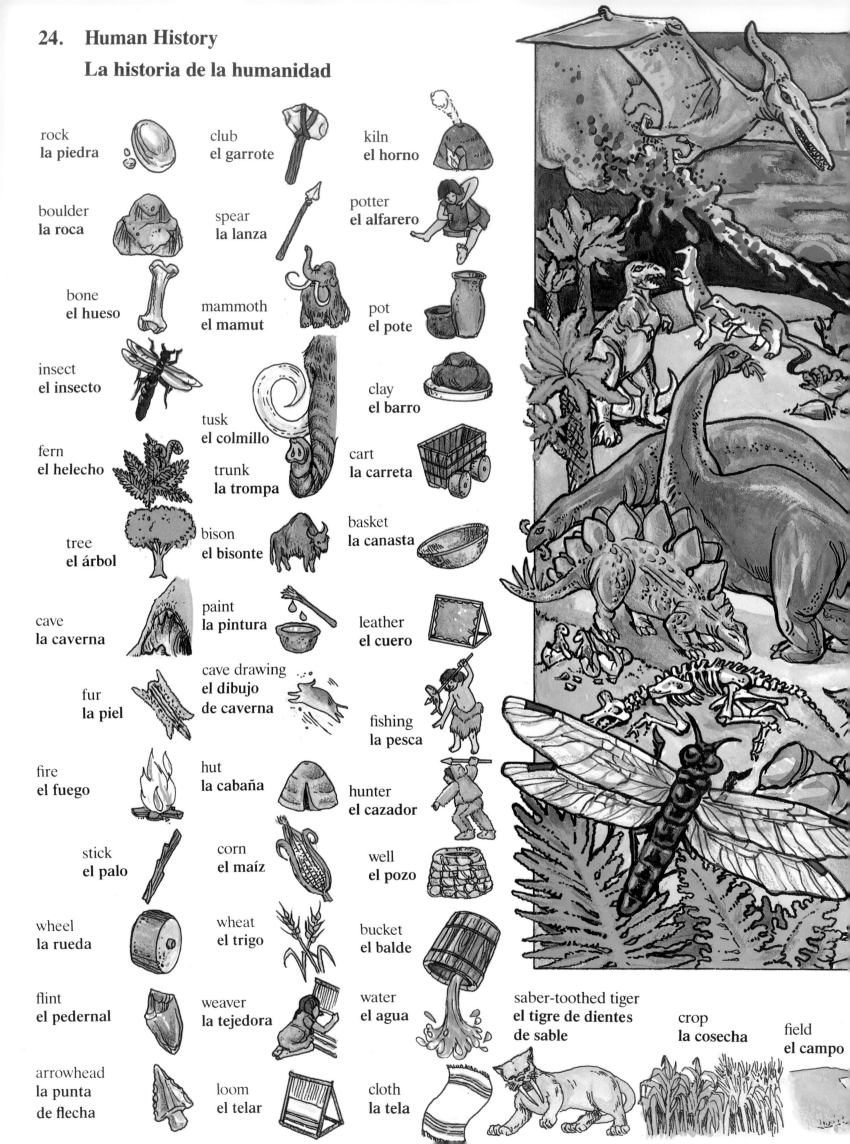

village
la aldea

cave dwellers
los cavernícolas

skeleton
el esqueleto

dinosaur
el dinosaurio

pterodactyl
el pterodáctilo

25. The Make-Believe Castle   El castillo de ficción

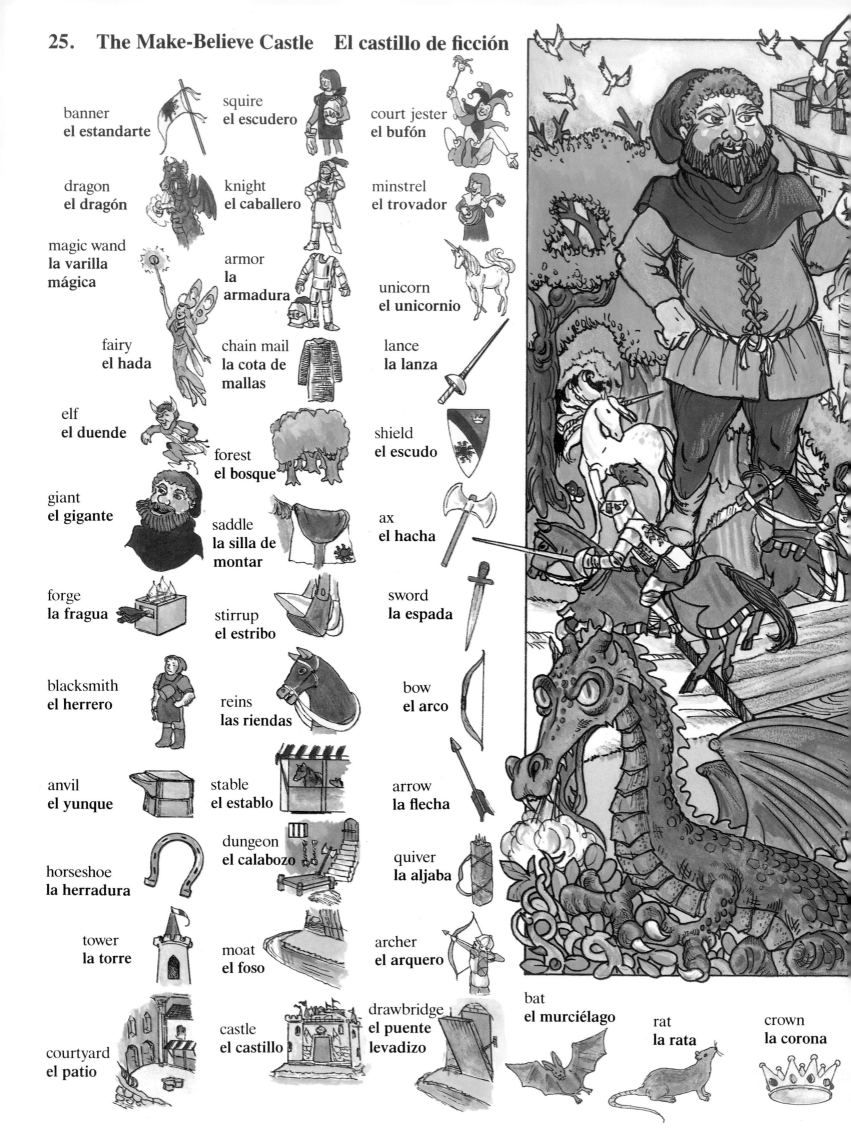

banner
el estandarte

dragon
el dragón

magic wand
la varilla mágica

fairy
el hada

elf
el duende

giant
el gigante

forge
la fragua

blacksmith
el herrero

anvil
el yunque

horseshoe
la herradura

tower
la torre

courtyard
el patio

squire
el escudero

knight
el caballero

armor
la armadura

chain mail
la cota de mallas

forest
el bosque

saddle
la silla de montar

stirrup
el estribo

reins
las riendas

stable
el establo

dungeon
el calabozo

moat
el foso

castle
el castillo

court jester
el bufón

minstrel
el trovador

unicorn
el unicornio

lance
la lanza

shield
el escudo

ax
el hacha

sword
la espada

bow
el arco

arrow
la flecha

quiver
la aljaba

archer
el arquero

drawbridge
el puente levadizo

bat
el murciélago

rat
la rata

crown
la corona

king
el rey

queen
la reina

princess
la princesa

prince
el príncipe

throne
el trono

spider
la araña

spiderweb
la telaraña

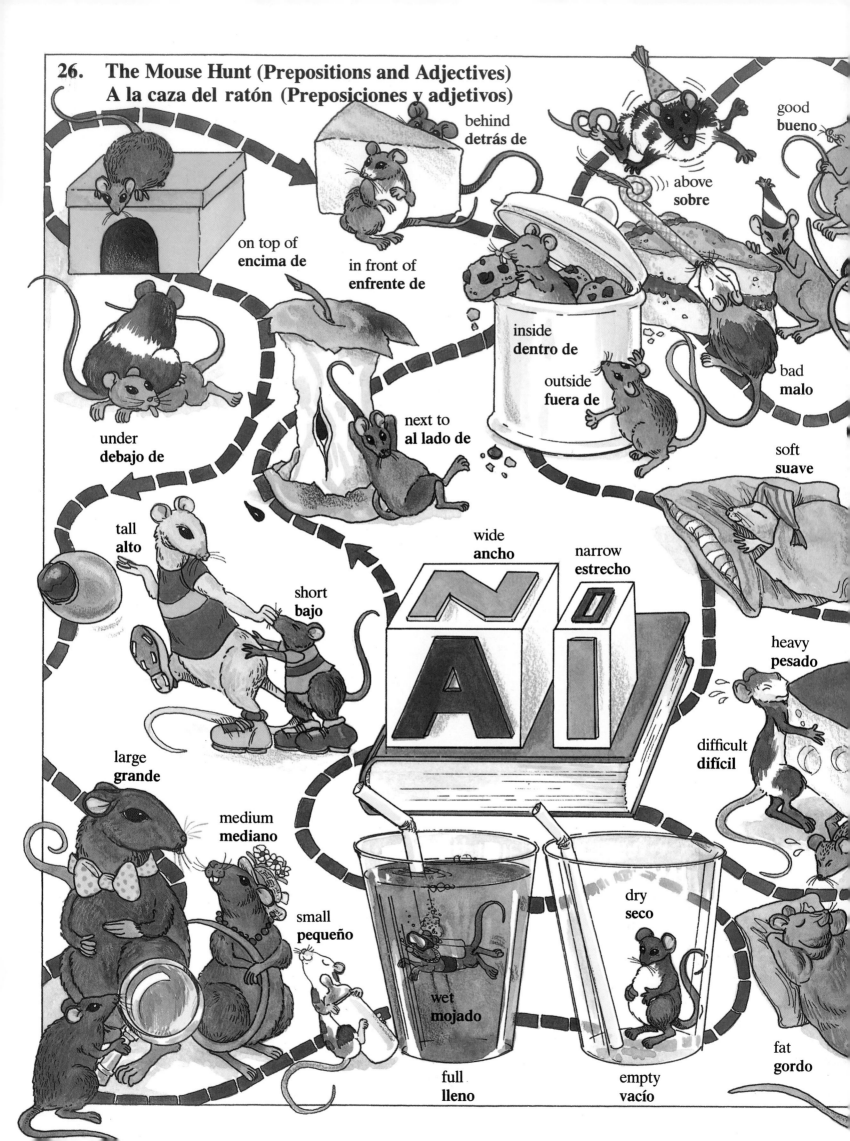

26. The Mouse Hunt (Prepositions and Adjectives)
A la caza del ratón (Preposiciones y adjetivos)

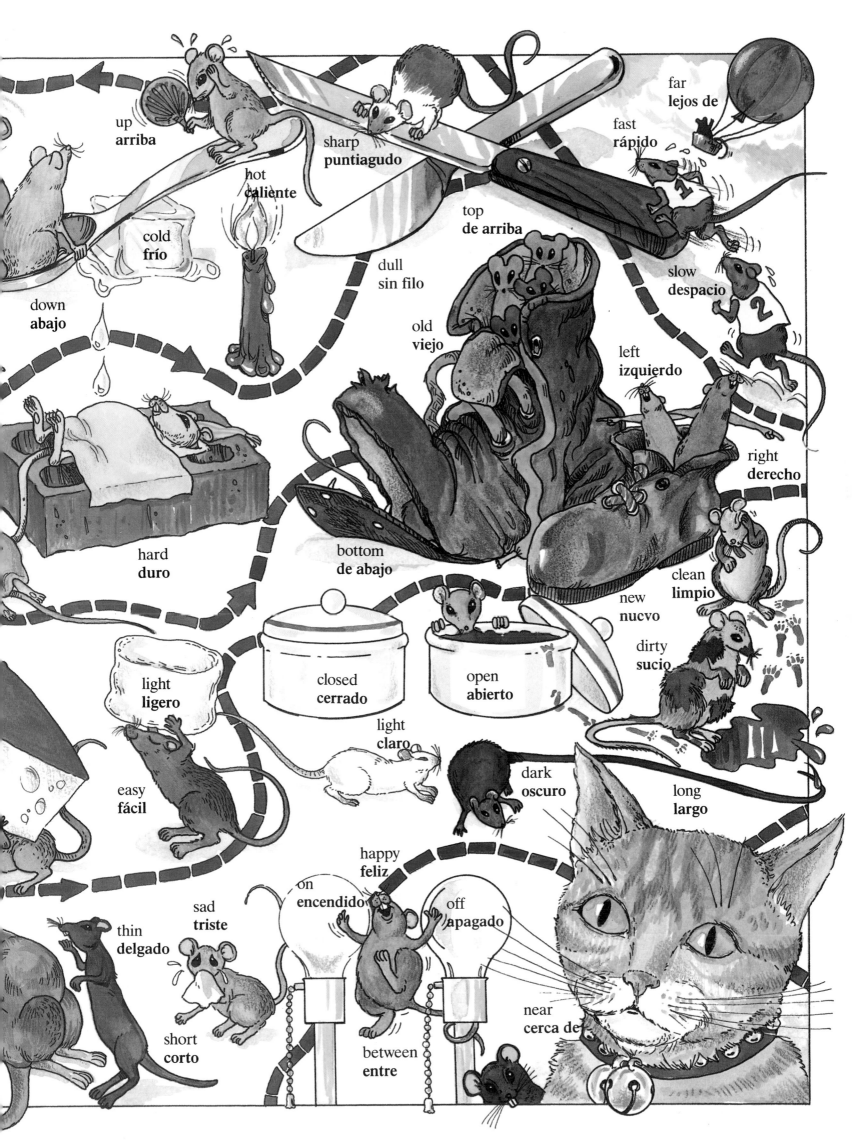

27. Action Words   Palabras de acción

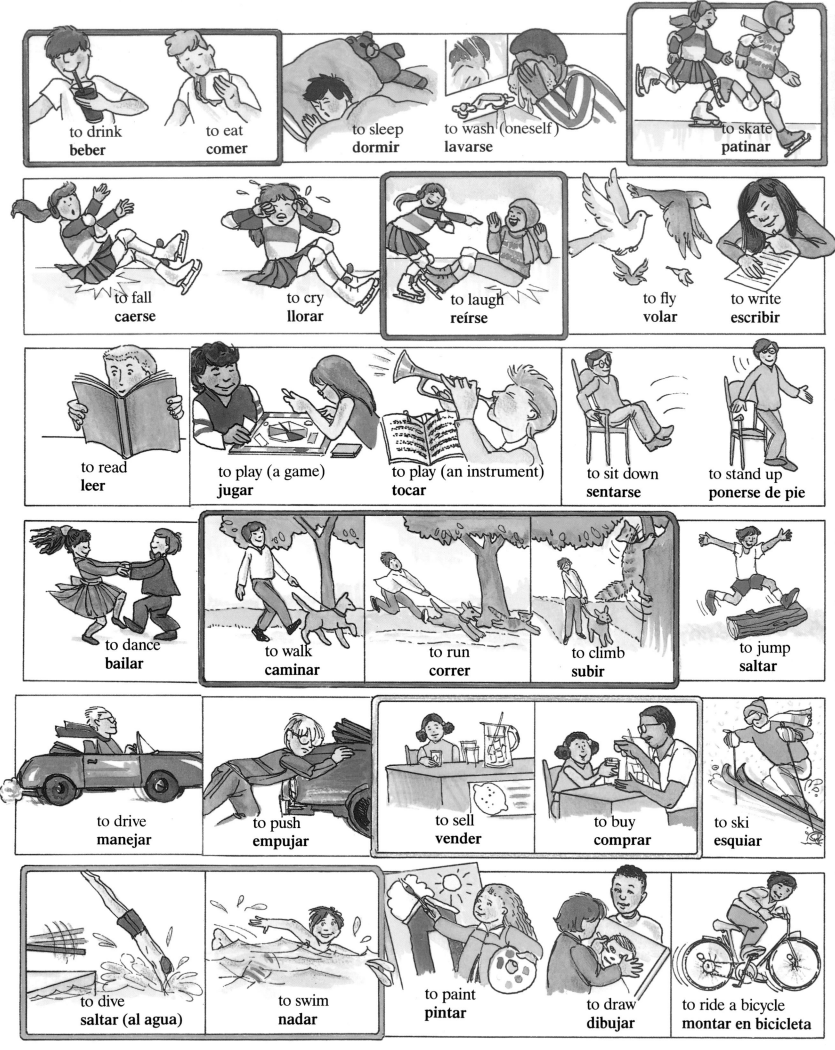

to drink
beber

to eat
comer

to sleep
dormir

to wash (oneself)
lavarse

to skate
patinar

to fall
caerse

to cry
llorar

to laugh
reírse

to fly
volar

to write
escribir

to read
leer

to play (a game)
jugar

to play (an instrument)
tocar

to sit down
sentarse

to stand up
ponerse de pie

to dance
bailar

to walk
caminar

to run
correr

to climb
subir

to jump
saltar

to drive
manejar

to push
empujar

to sell
vender

to buy
comprar

to ski
esquiar

to dive
saltar (al agua)

to swim
nadar

to paint
pintar

to draw
dibujar

to ride a bicycle
montar en bicicleta

to come
venir

to go
ir

to throw
tirar

to catch
recoger

to watch
mirar

to sing
cantar

to talk
hablar

to kick
patear

to listen (to)
escuchar

to think
pensar

to roar
rugir

to dig
cavar

to water
regar

to juggle
hacer juegos malabares

to point (at)
señalar

to look for
buscar

to find
encontrar

to give
dar

to receive
recibir

to cut
cortar

to cook
cocinar

to open
abrir

to close
cerrar

to take a bath
bañarse

to teach
enseñar

to break
romper

to fix
arreglar

to carry
llevar

to pull
tirar

to wait
esperar

28. Colors   Los colores

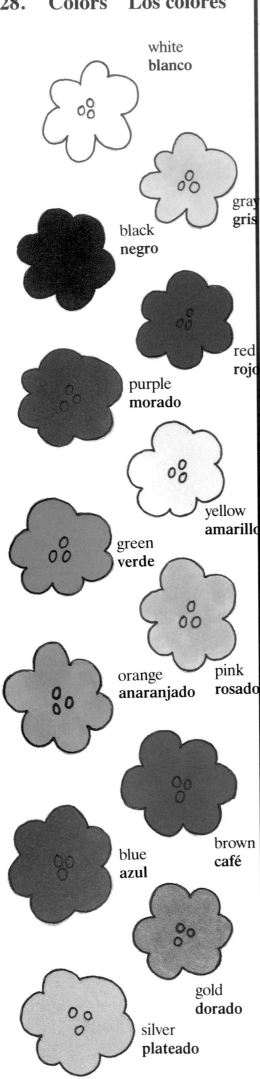

white
blanco

gray
gris

black
negro

red
rojo

purple
morado

yellow
amarillo

green
verde

orange
anaranjado

pink
rosado

blue
azul

brown
café

gold
dorado

silver
plateado

29. The Family Tree   El árbol genealógico

grandmother, grandma
la abuela, la abuelita

mother, mom
**la madre,
la mamá**

father, dad
el padre, el papá

son
el hijo

brother
el hermano

sister
la hermana

grandfather, grandpa
el abuelo, el abuelito

uncle **el tío**

aunt **la tía**

cousin **el primo**

cousin **la prima**

daughter **la hija**

30. Shapes   Las formas

square **el cuadrado**

triangle **el triángulo**

circle **el círculo**

rectangle   **el rectángulo**

oval **el óvalo**

cube **el cubo**

octagon **el octágono**

sphere **la esfera**

cylinder **el cilindro**

cone **el cono**

31. Numbers Los números

Ordinal Numbers
Los números ordinales

tenth
décimo

ninth
noveno

eighth
octavo

sixth
sexto

seventh
séptimo

fifth
quinto

fourth
cuarto

second
segundo

third
tercero

first
primero

Cardinal Numbers
Los números cardinales

0 zero **cero**	½ one-half **la mitad**	1 one **uno**	2 two **dos**	3 three **tres**	4 four **cuatro**	5 five **cinco**	6 six **seis**

16 sixteen **dieciséis**	17 seventeen **diecisiete**	18 eighteen **dieciocho**	19 nineteen **diecinueve**	20 twenty **veinte**	21 twenty-one **veintiuno**

28 twenty-eight **veintiocho**	29 twenty-nine **veintinueve**	30 thirty **treinta**	31 thirty-one **treinta y uno**

37 thirty-seven **treinta y siete**	38 thirty-eight **treinta y ocho**	39 thirty-nine **treinta y nueve**	40 forty **cuarenta**

46 forty-six **cuarenta y seis**	47 forty-seven **cuarenta y siete**	48 forty-eight **cuarenta y ocho**	49 forty-nine **cuarenta y nueve**

55 fifty-five **cincuenta y cinco**	56 fifty-six **cincuenta y seis**	57 fifty-seven **cincuenta y siete**	58 fifty-eight **cincuenta y ocho**

64 sixty-four **sesenta y cuatro**	65 sixty-five **sesenta y cinco**	66 sixty-six **sesenta y seis**	67 sixty-seven **sesenta y siete**

73 seventy-three **setenta y tres**	74 seventy-four **setenta y cuatro**	75 seventy-five **setenta y cinco**	76 seventy-six **setenta y seis**

82 eighty-two **ochenta y dos**	83 eighty-three **ochenta y tres**	84 eighty-four **ochenta y cuatro**	85 eighty-five **ochenta y cinco**

91 ninety-one **noventa y uno**	92 ninety-two **noventa y dos**	93 ninety-three **noventa y tres**	94 ninety-four **noventa y cuatro**

100 one hundred **cien**	1,000 one thousand **mil**	10,000 ten thousand **diez mil**

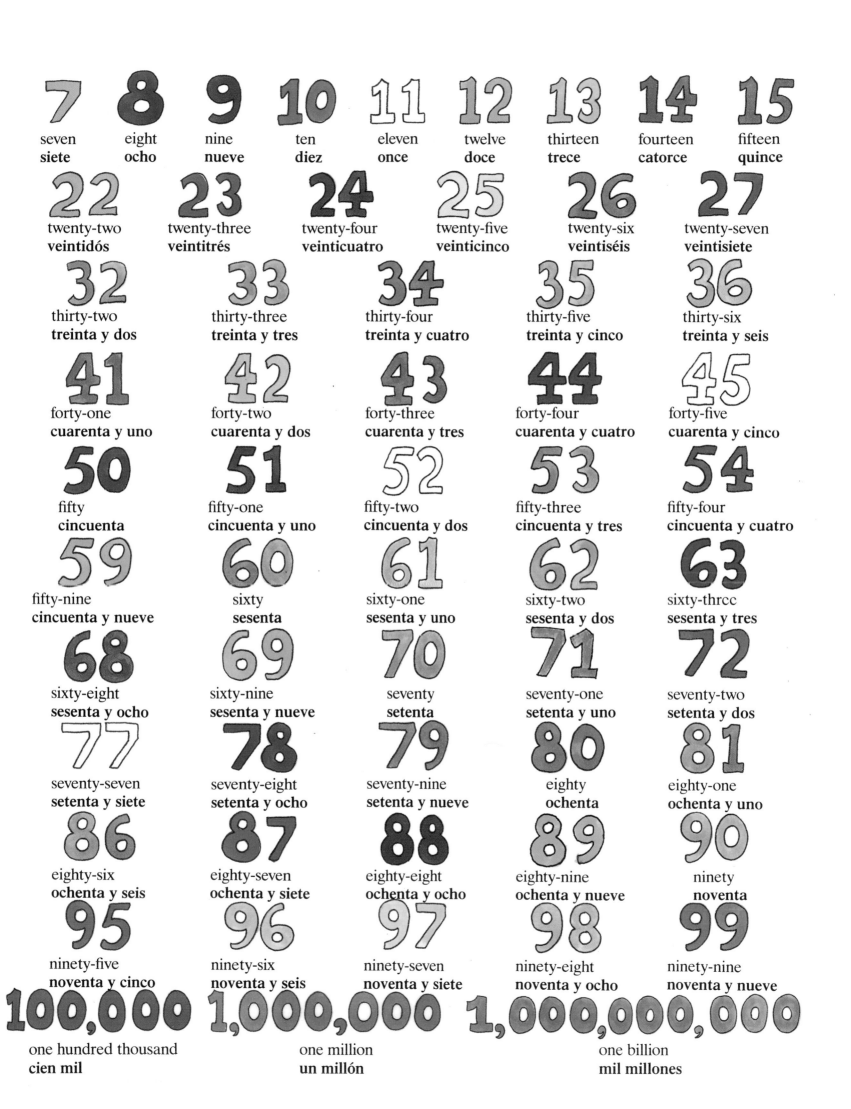

7 seven / siete

8 eight / ocho

9 nine / nueve

10 ten / diez

11 eleven / once

12 twelve / doce

13 thirteen / trece

14 fourteen / catorce

15 fifteen / quince

22 twenty-two / veintidós

23 twenty-three / veintitrés

24 twenty-four / veinticuatro

25 twenty-five / veinticinco

26 twenty-six / veintiséis

27 twenty-seven / veintisiete

32 thirty-two / treinta y dos

33 thirty-three / treinta y tres

34 thirty-four / treinta y cuatro

35 thirty-five / treinta y cinco

36 thirty-six / treinta y seis

41 forty-one / cuarenta y uno

42 forty-two / cuarenta y dos

43 forty-three / cuarenta y tres

44 forty-four / cuarenta y cuatro

45 forty-five / cuarenta y cinco

50 fifty / cincuenta

51 fifty-one / cincuenta y uno

52 fifty-two / cincuenta y dos

53 fifty-three / cincuenta y tres

54 fifty-four / cincuenta y cuatro

59 fifty-nine / cincuenta y nueve

60 sixty / sesenta

61 sixty-one / sesenta y uno

62 sixty-two / sesenta y dos

63 sixty-three / sesenta y tres

68 sixty-eight / sesenta y ocho

69 sixty-nine / sesenta y nueve

70 seventy / setenta

71 seventy-one / setenta y uno

72 seventy-two / setenta y dos

77 seventy-seven / setenta y siete

78 seventy-eight / setenta y ocho

79 seventy-nine / setenta y nueve

80 eighty / ochenta

81 eighty-one / ochenta y uno

86 eighty-six / ochenta y seis

87 eighty-seven / ochenta y siete

88 eighty-eight / ochenta y ocho

89 eighty-nine / ochenta y nueve

90 ninety / noventa

95 ninety-five / noventa y cinco

96 ninety-six / noventa y seis

97 ninety-seven / noventa y siete

98 ninety-eight / noventa y ocho

99 ninety-nine / noventa y nueve

100,000 one hundred thousand / cien mil

1,000,000 one million / un millón

1,000,000,000 one billion / mil millones

32. A Map of the World   Un mapamundi

Arctic Ocean
el Océano Glacial Ártico

bay
la bahía

glacier
el glaciar

iceberg
el témpano

lake
el lago

North America
la América del Norte

channel
el canal

fault
la falla

plain
la llanura

Atlantic Ocean
el Océano Atlántico

gulf
el golfo

desert
el desierto

Pacific Ocean
el Océano Pacífico

canal
el canal

equator
el ecuador

jungle
la selva

compass
la brújula

north
norte

northwest
noroeste

northeast
nordeste

South America
la América del Sur

west
oeste

east
este

southwest
sudoeste

southeast
sudeste

south
sur

cape
el cabo

icecap
el manto de hielo

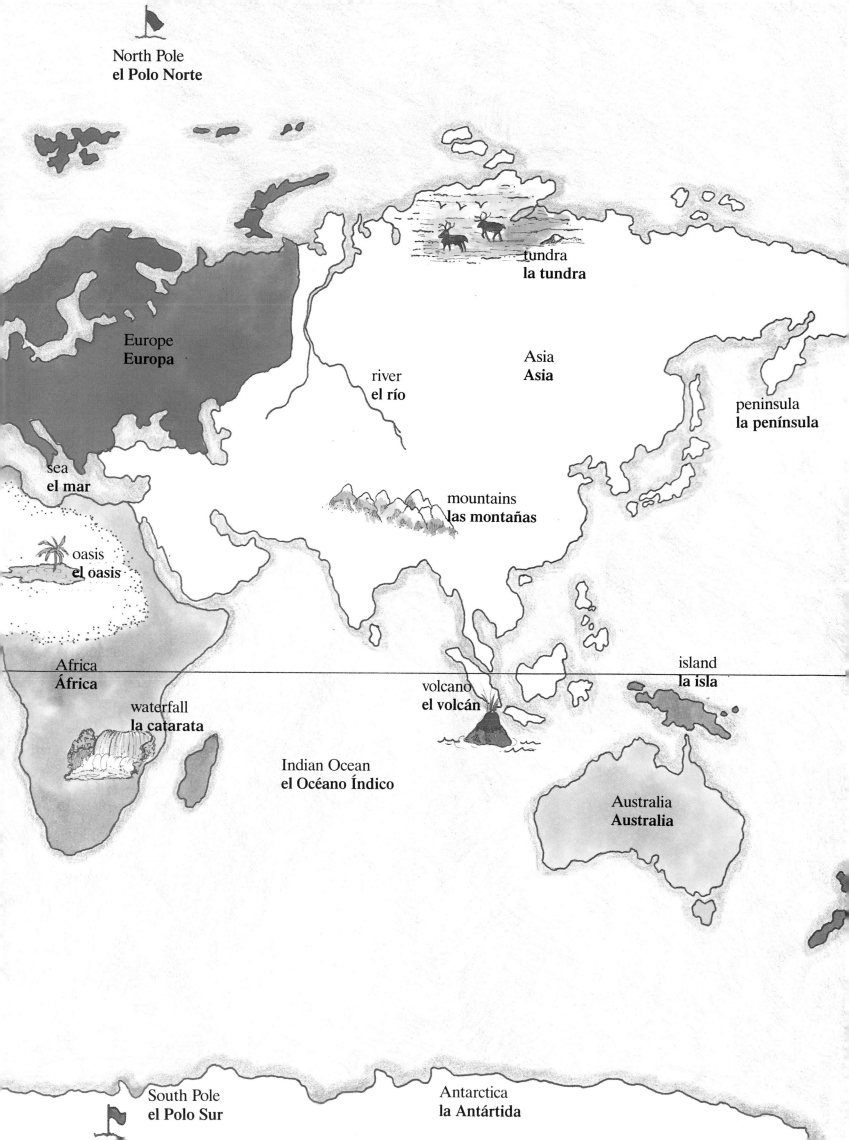

North Pole
el Polo Norte

tundra
la tundra

Europe
Europa

Asia
Asia

river
el río

peninsula
la península

sea
el mar

mountains
las montañas

oasis
el oasis

Africa
África

island
la isla

waterfall
la catarata

volcano
el volcán

Indian Ocean
el Océano Índico

Australia
Australia

South Pole
el Polo Sur

Antarctica
la Antártida

Spanish-English Glossary and Index

How to Say the Words in Spanish

One of the most difficult things about learning a new language is pronunciation, how to say the words in the language. That's why we've written pronunciation guides to help you say the words in this book correctly. You will find a pronunciation guide in parentheses after each Spanish word in the *Spanish-English Glossary and Index*. It may look funny, but if you read it aloud, you will be saying the word correctly.

Here are a few hints about saying words in Spanish. The Spanish *r* is different from the English *r*. To say it correctly, "trill" the sound by flapping your tongue against the roof of your mouth once. Whenever you see *rr* in a pronunciation guide, trill the sound longer by flapping your tongue against the roof of your mouth several times. The Spanish letter *ñ* is pronounced "ny." You will see it written as "ny" in the pronunciation guides. The letter *ll* is pronounced as "y" and that's how you will see it written in the pronunciation guides. The letter *a* is written as "ah" in the pronunciation guides and always sounds like the *a* in *father*. The letter "o" always sounds like the *o* in *go*. And remember to always pronounce the letter *e* like the *e* in *let*, even when it comes before the letter *r*.

You will also see that each word in the pronunciation guides has one syllable in heavy black letters. This is the stressed syllable. When you say a word in English, you always say one syllable a little louder than the others. This is called the stressed syllable. When you read the pronunciation guides aloud, just say the syllable in heavy dark letters a little louder than the others to use the correct stress.

Alphabetical order is also a little different in Spanish because the *ch*, *ll*, and *ñ* are considered separate letters. So words that begin with *ch* come after all words that begin with *c*, words that begin with *ll* come after all words that begin with *l*, and words that begin with *ñ* come after all words that begin with *n*. For example, in this glossary, *el champú* comes after *la cuna*, *la llanta* comes after *la luna*, and *el moño* comes after *montar*.

After the pronunciation guide, the *Spanish-English Glossary and Index* gives the English meaning for each word and the number of the picture where you can find that word.

abajo (ah-**bah**-ho), down, 26
de abajo (day ah-**bah**-ho), bottom, 26
el abanico (el ah-bah-**nee**-ko), fan, 4
las abejas (lahs ah-**bay**-has), bees, 9
abierto (ah-**byer**-to) open, 26
la abogada (lah ah-bo-**gah**-dah), lawyer, 15
el abrigo (el ah-**bree**-go), coat, 7
abrir (ah-**breer**), open, 27
la abuela (lah ah-**bway**-lah), grandmother, 29
la abuelita (lah ah-bway-**lee**-tah), grandma, 29
el abuelito (el ah-bway-**lee**-to), grandpa, 29
el abuelo (el ah-**bway**-lo), grandfather, 29
la acción (lah ahk-**syon**), action, 27
el aceite (el ah-**say**-tay), oil, 14
la acera (lah ah-**say**-rah), sidewalk, 16
el acordeón (el ah-kor-day-**on**), accordion, 19
el acróbata (el ah-**kro**-bah-tah), acrobat, 21
el actor (el ahk-**tor**), actor, 19
la actriz (lah ahk-**trees**), actress, 19
el acuario (el ah-**kwah**-ryo), aquarium, 1
¡Adelante! (ah-day-**lahn**-tay), Go!, 16
los adjetivos (los ad-hay-**tee**-vos), adjectives, 26
la aduanera (lah ah-dwah-**nay**-rah), customs officer, 17
el aeropuerto (el ah-ay-ro-**pwer**-to), airport, 17
África (**ah**-free-kah), Africa, 32
las agallas (lahs ah-**gah**-yas), gills, 22
el agua (el **ah**-gwah), water, 24
el aguacate (el ah-gwah-**kah**-tay), avocado, 6
el águila (el **ah**-gee-lah), eagle, 20
la aguja hipodérmica (lah ah-**goo**-hah ee-po-**der**-mee-kah) hypodermic needle, 11
las agujas de tejer (lahs ah-**goo**-hahs day **tay**-her), knitting needles, 4
el ajedrez (el ah-hay-**dres**), chess, 4
el ala (el **ah**-lah), wing, 17
las alas (lahs **ah**-lahs), wings, 20
el álbum de fotos (el **al**-boom day **fo**-tos), photo album, 4
la aleta (lah ah-**lay**-tah), fin, 22; flipper, 22
el alfabeto (el ahl-fah-**bay**-to), alphabet, 1
el alfarero (el ahl-fah-**ray**-ro), potter, 24
la alfombra (lah ahl-**fom**-brah), carpet, rug, 1, 2

el alga marina (el **ahl**-gah mah-**ree**-nah), seaweed, 22
el algodón de azúcar (el ahl-go-**don** day ah-**soo**-kar), cotton candy, 21
los alicates (los ah-lee-**kah**-tes), pliers, 14
la aljaba (lah ahl-**hah**-bah), quiver, 25
el almacén (el ahl-mah-**sen**), clothing store, 8
la almeja (lah ahl-**may**-hah), clam, 22
la almohada (lah ahl-mo-**ah**-dah), pillow, 2
el almuerzo (el ahl-**mwer**-so), lunch, 10
el altavoz (el ahl-tah-**bos**), loudspeaker, 1
¡Alto! (**ahl**-to), Stop!, 16
alto (**ahl**-to), tall, 26
la alumnna (lah ah-**loom**-nah), student (female), 1
el alumno (el ah-**loom**-no), student (male), 1
amarillo (ah-mah-**ree**-yo), yellow, 28
la ambulancia (lah ahm-boo-**lahn**-syah), ambulance, 16
la América del Norte (lah ah-**may**-ree-kah del **nor**-tay), North America, 32
la América del Sur (lah ah-**may**-ree-kah del **soor**), South America, 32
anaranjado (ah-nah-rahn-**hah**-do), orange, 28
el ancla (el **ahn**-klah), anchor, 22
ancho (**ahn**-cho), wide, 26
el angelote (el ahn-hay-**lo**-tay), angelfish, 22
los anillos (los ah-**nee**-yos), rings, 23
el animador (el ah-nee-mah-**dor**), master of ceremonies, 19
los animales (los ah-nee-**mah**-les), animals, 20
la Antártida (lah ahn-**tar**-tee-dah), Antarctica, 32
la antena (lah ahn-**tay**-nah), antenna, 23
los anteojos (los ahn-tay-**o**-hos), glasses, 7
los anteojos de sol (los ahn-tay-**o**-hos day **sol**), sunglasses, 7
el anzuelo (el ahn-**swe**-lo), fishhook, 22
apagado (ah-pah-**gah**-do), off, 26
el aparcamiento (el ah-par-kah-**myen**-to), parking lot, 8
el apartado postal (el ah-pahr-**tah**-do pos-**tahl**), post-office box, 13
el apio (el **ah**-pyo), celery, 10

la araña (lah ah-**rah**-nyah), spider, 25
el árbitro (el **ar**-bee-tro), referee, umpire, 18
el árbol (el **ar**-bol), tree, 9, 24
el árbol genealógico (el **ar**-bol hay-nay-ah-**lo**-hee-ko), family tree, 29
el arbusto (el ar-**boos**-to), bush, 5
el arca de tesoro (el **ar**-kah day tay-**so**-ro), treasure chest, 22
el archivo (el ar-**chee**-bo), file cabinet, 13
el arco (el **ar**-ko), bow (for a violin), 19; (weapon), 25
el arco iris (el **ar**-ko ee-rees), rainbow, 5
la arena (lah ah-**ray**-nah), sand, 22
el arete (el ah-**ray**-tay), earring, 7
la armadura (lah ar-mah-**doo**-rah), armor, 25
el aro (el **ah**-ro), hoop, 21
el arpa (el **ar**-pah), harp, 19
el arquero (el ar-**kay**-ro), archer, 25
la arquitecta (lah ar-kee-**tek**-tah), architect, 15
la artista (lah ar-**tees**-tah), artist, 15
el arrecife de coral (el ah-**rray**-**see**-fay day ko-**rahl**), coral reef, 22
arreglar (ah-rray-**glar**), fix, 27
arriba (ah-**rree**-bah), up, 26
de arriba (day ah-**rree**-bah), top, 26
el arroz (el ah-**rros**), rice, 10
el ascensor (el ahs-sen-**sor**), elevator, 17
Asia (**ah**-sya), Asia, 32
el asiento (el ah-**syen**-to), seat, 17
el asiento del conductor (el ah-**syen**-to del kon-dook-**tor**), driver's seat, 14
el asiento del pasajero (el ah-**syen**-to del pah-sah-**hay**-ro), passenger's seat, 14
el asiento posterior (el ah-**syen**-to pos-tay-**ryor**), backseat, 14
la aspiradora (lah ahs-pee-rah-**do**-rah), vacuum cleaner, 3
el asteroide (el ahs-tay-**roy**-day), asteroid, 23
el astronauta (el ahs-tro-**now**-tah), astronaut, 23
el astrónomo (el ahs-**tro**-no-mo), astronomer, 15
el atleta (el aht-**lay**-tah), athlete, 15
el auditorio (el ow-dee-**to**-ryo), auditorium, 19

el **aula** (el **ow**-lah), classroom, 1
Australia (ows-**trah**-lya), Australia, 32
el **autobús** (el ow-to-**boos**), bus, 16
el **autobús escolar** (el ow-to-**boos** es-ko-**lar**), school bus, 16
el **auxiliar del médico** (el ow-gsee-**lyar** del **may**-dee-ko), paramedic, 15
el **auxiliar de vuelo** (el ow-gsee-**lyar** day **bwe**-lo), flight attendant, 17
el **avestruz** (el ah-bes-**troos**), ostrich, 20
el **avión** (el ah-**byon**), airplane, 16, 17
el **azúcar** (el ah-**soo**-kar), sugar, 10
azul (ah-**sool**), blue, 28

el **badminton** (el **bad**-meen-ton), badminton, 18
la **bahía** (lah bah-**ee**-ah), bay, 32
bailar (bigh-**lar**), dance, 27
la **bailarina** (lah bigh-lah-**ree**-nah), dancer, 19
bajo (**bah**-ho), short, 26
la **balanza** (lah bah-**lahn**-sah), scale, 13
el **balcón** (el bahl-**kon**), balcony, 8
el **balde** (el **bahl**-day), bucket, 24
el **baloncesto** (el bah-lon-**ses**-to), basketball, 18
la **ballena** (lah bah-**yay**-nah), whale, 22
el **banco** (el **ban**-ko), bank, 13; bench, 8; school (of fish), 22
la **banda** (lah **bahn**-dah), band, 21
la **bandeja** (lah bahn-**day**-hah), tray, 10
las **banderas** (lahs bahn-**day**-ras), flags, 17
la **banquera** (lah bahn-**kay**-rah), banker, 15
el **banquillo** (el bahn-**kee**-yo), footstool, 2
bañarse (bah-**nyar**-say), take a bath, 27
los **baños** (los **bah**-nyos), rest rooms, 21
la **barba** (lah **bar**-bah), beard, 12
la **barbacoa** (lah bar-bah-**ko**-ah), barbecue, 5
el **barbero** (el bar-**bay**-ro), barber, 12
la **barbilla** (lah bar-**bee**-ya), chin, 11
el **barco** (el **bar**-ko), boat, 16
el **barco de vela** (el **bar**-ko day **bay**-lah), sailboat, 16
el **barco remolcador** (el **bar**-ko rray-mol-kah-**dor**), tugboat, 16
las **barras** (lahs **bah**-rras), jungle gym, 8
el **barro** (el **bah**-rro), clay, 24
la **báscula** (lah **bahs**-koo-lah), scale, 6
el **bastón** (el bahs-**ton**), cane, 11
la **basura** (lah bah-**soo**-rah), trash, 1
la **bata** (lah **bah**-tah), bathrobe, 7
la **bata de laboratorio** (lah **bah**-tah day lah-bo-rah-**to**-ryo), lab coat, 23
el **bate** (el **bah**-tay), bat, 18
la **batidora eléctrica** (lah bah-tee-**do**-rah ay-**lek**-tree-kah), electric mixer, 3
el **baúl** (el bah-**ool**), trunk (luggage), 4; (car), 14
el **bebé** (el bay-**bay**), baby, 9
beber (bay-**ber**), drink, 27
el **becerro** (el bay-**say**-rro), calf, 9
el **béisbol** (el **bays**-bol), baseball, 18
el **bibliotecario** (el bee-blyo-tay-**kah**-ryo), librarian, 15
la **bicicleta** (lah bee-see-**klay**-tah), bicycle, 14, 16, 18
el **bigote** (el bee-**go**-tay), mustache, 12
el **billete** (el bee-**yay**-tay), bill, 13
la **billetera** (lah bee-yay-**tay**-rah), wallet, 13
el **bisonte** (el bee-**son**-tay), bison, 24
el **bistec** (el bees-**tek**), steak, 10
blanco (**blahn**-ko), white, 28
la **blusa** (lah **bloo**-sah), blouse, 7
la **boca** (lah **bo**-kah), mouth, 11
la **boca de incendios** (lah **bo**-kah day een-**sen**-dyos), fire hydrant, 8
el **bocadillo** (el bo-kah-**dee**-yo), sandwich, 10
la **bola de nieve** (lah **bo**-lah day **nyay**-bay), snowball, 5
el **boleto** (el bo-**lay**-to), ticket, 17
el **bolígrafo** (el bo-**lee**-grah-fo), pen, 1
la **bolsa de compras** (lah **bol**-sah day **kom**-pras), shopping bag, 6
la **bolsa de correo** (lah **bol**-sah day ko-**rray**-o), mailbag, 13
el **bolsillo** (el bol-**see**-yo), pocket, 7
el **bolso** (el **bol**-so), purse, 17
el **bombero** (el bom-**bay**-ro), fire fighter, 15
la **bombilla** (lah bom-**bee**-yah), lightbulb, 4, 21
el **borrador** (el bo-**rrah**-dor), eraser (chalkboard), 1
el **bosque** (el **bos**-kay), forest, 25
las **botas** (lahs **bo**-tahs), boots, 7
las **botas de campo** (lahs **bo**-tahs day **kam**-po), hiking boots, 7
las **botas de vaquero** (lahs **bo**-tahs day bah-**kay**-ro), cowboy boots, 4
el **bote de remos** (el **bo**-tay day **ray**-mos), rowboat, 16
la **botella** (lah bo-**tay**-ya), bottle, 6
el **botón** (el bo-**ton**), button, 7
el **boxeo** (el bo-**gsay**-o), boxing, 18
la **boya** (lah **bo**-yah), buoy, 22
el **brazo** (el **brah**-so), arm, 11
el **bróculi** (el **bro**-koo-lee), broccoli, 10
la **brújula** (lah **broo**-hoo-lah), compass, 32
el **buceador** (el boo-say-ah-**dor**), scuba diver, 22
bueno (**bway**-no), good, 26
la **bufanda** (lah boo-**fahn**-dah), scarf, 7
el **bufón** (el boo-**fon**), court jester, 25
la **burbuja** (lah boor-**boo**-hah), bubble, 22
el **burro** (el **boo**-rro), donkey, 9
buscar (boos-**kar**), look for, 27
el **buzón** (el boo-**son**), mailbox, 13

el **caballero** (el kah-bah-**yay**-ro), knight, 25
el **caballete de pintor** (el kah-bah-**yay**-tay day peen-**tor**), easel, 1
el **caballo** (el kah-**bah**-yo), horse, 9
el **caballo mecedor** (el kah-**bah**-yo may-say-**dor**), rocking horse, 4
la **cabaña** (lah kah-**bah**-nyah), hut, 24
el **cabestrillo** (el kah-bes-**tree**-yo), sling, 11
la **cabeza** (lah kah-**bay**-sah), head, 11
la **cabina telefónica** (lah kah-**bee**-nah tay-lay-**fo**-nee-kah), phone booth, 13
el **cabo** (el **kah**-bo), cape, 32
la **cabra** (lah **kah**-brah), goat, 9
los **cacahuates** (los kah-kah-**wah**-tes), peanuts, 21
el **cacto** (el **kahk**-to), cactus, 1
el **cachorro** (el kah-**cho**-rro), puppy, 9
el **cachorro de oso** (el kah-**cho**-rro day **o**-so), bear cub, 20
el **cachorro de tigre** (el kah-**cho**-rro day **tee**-gray), tiger cub, 20
la **cadena de bicicleta** (lah kah-**day**-nah day bee-see-**klay**-tah), bicycle chain, 14
caerse (kah-**er**-say), fall, 27
café (kah-**fay**), brown, 28
el **café** (el kah-**fay**), coffee, 10
la **cafetería** (lah kah-fay-tay-**ree**-ah), snack bar, 17
el **caimán** (el kigh-**mahn**), alligator, 20
la **caja** (lah **kah**-hah), box, 4; cash register, 6
la **caja de herramientas** (lah **kah**-hah day ay-rrah-**myen**-tahs), toolbox, 3
la **caja de seguridad** (lah **kah**-hah day say-goo-ree-**dahd**), safety deposit box, 13
la **caja fuerte** (lah **kah**-hah **fwer**-tay), safe, 13
la **cajera** (lah kah-**hay**-rah), cashier, teller, 6, 13
el **cajero automático** (el kah-**hay**-ro ow-to-**mah**-tee-ko), automatic teller, 13
la **cajita de música** (lah kah-**hee**-tah day **moo**-see-kah), music box, 4
el **cajón** (el kah-**hon**), drawer, 3
el **cajón de arena** (el kah-**hon** day ah-**ray**-nah), sandbox, 8
el **calabozo** (el kah-lah-**bo**-so), dungeon, 25
el **calamar** (el kah-lah-**mar**), squid, 22
los **calcetines** (los kahl-say-**tee**-nes), socks, 7
la **calculadora** (lah kahl-koo-lah-**do**-rah), calculator, 1
el **calendario** (el kah-len-**dah**-ryo), calendar, 1
caliente (kah-**lyen**-tay), hot, 26
calvo (**kal**-bo), bald, 12
la **calle** (lah **kah**-yay), street, 16
la **cama** (lah **kah**-mah), bed, 2
la **cámara** (lah **kah**-mah-rah), camera, 17, 21
la **cámara de seguridad** (lah **kah**-mah-rah day say-goo-ree-**dahd**), security camera, 13
la **cámara de video** (lah **kah**-mah-rah day **bee**-day-o), video camera, 17
la **camarera** (lah kah-mah-**ray**-rah), waitress, 10
el **camarero** (el kah-mah-**ray**-ro), waiter, 10
el **camarín** (el kah-mah-**reen**), dressing room, 19
el **camello** (el kah-**may**-yo), camel, 20
la **camilla** (lah kah-**mee**-ya), examining table, 11
caminar (kah-mee-**nar**), walk, 27
el **caminar en el espacio** (el kah-mee-**nar** en el es-**pah**-syo), space walk, 23
el **camino** (el kah-**mee**-no), road, 9
el **camino particular** (el kah-**mee**-no par-tee-koo-**lar**), driveway, 8
el **camión** (el kah-**myon**), truck, 16
el **camión tanque** (el kah-**myon** tan-kay), tank truck, 14
el **camionero** (el kah-myo-**nay**-ro), truck driver, 14
la **camioneta** (lah kah-myo-**nay**-tah), van, 16
la **camisa** (lah kah-**mee**-sah), shirt, 7
la **camisa de entrenamiento** (lah kah-**mee**-sah day en-tray-nah-**myen**-to), sweatshirt, 7
la **camiseta** (lah kah-mee-**say**-tah), T-shirt, 7
la **campana** (lah kam-**pah**-nah), bell, 1
el **campo** (el **kam**-po), country, 9; field, 24
el **canal** (el kah-**nahl**), canal, channel, 32
la **canasta** (lah kah-**nahs**-tah), basket, 24
el **cangrejo** (el kahn-**gray**-ho), crab, 22
el **canguro** (el kahn-**goo**-ro), kangaroo, 20
las **canicas** (lahs kah-**nee**-kahs), marbles, 4
la **canoa** (lah kah-**no**-ah), canoe, 16
el **cantante** (el kahn-**tahn**-tay), singer, 19
cantar (kahn-**tar**), sing, 27
el **cañón** (el kah-**nyon**), cannon, 22
la **capa** (lah **kah**-pah), cape, 21
el **capataz** (el kah-pah-**tas**), foreman, 15
el **capó** (el kah-**po**), hood, 14
la **cápsula de aterrizaje** (lah **kap**-soo-lah day ah-tay-rree-**sah**-hay), landing capsule, 23
la **capucha** (lah kah-**poo**-chah), hood, 7
la **cara** (lah **kah**-rah), face, 11
el **carámbano** (el kah-**ram**-bah-no), icicle, 5
la **caravana** (lah kah-rah-**bah**-nah), camper, 16
la **cárcel** (lah **kar**-sel), jail, 8
la **carne** (lah **kar**-nay), meat, 6
la **carnicería** (lah kar-nee-say-**ree**-ah), butcher shop, 8
el **carnicero** (el kar-nee-**say**-ro), butcher, 15
el **carpintero** (el kar-peen-**tay**-ro), carpenter, 15
las **carreras de caballos** (lahs kah-**rray**-ras day kah-**bah**-yos), horse racing, 18
las **carreras de coches** (lahs kah-**rray**-ras day **ko**-ches), car racing, 18
la **carreta** (lah kah-**rray**-tah), cart, 24
el **carrito de compras** (el kah-**rree**-to day **kom**-prahs), shopping cart, 6

el carrito de equipaje (el kah-**rree**-to day ay-kee-**pah**-hay), baggage cart, 17

el carro de nieve (el **kah**-rro day **nyay**-bay), snowmobile, 5

la carta (lah **kar**-tah), letter, 13

el cartel (el kar-**tel**), poster, 2

la cartera (lah kar-**tay**-rah), briefcase, 17

el cartero (el kar-**tay**-ro), letter carrier, 15

la casa (lah **kah**-sah), house, 2

la casa de muñecas (lah **kah**-sah day moo-**nyay**-kahs), dollhouse, 4

el casco (el **kahs**-ko), helmet, 18; hoof, 20

el casco del tanque de gasolina (el **kahs**-ko del **tan**-kay day gah-so-**lee**-nah), gas cap, 14

el casco espacial (el **kahs**-ko es-pah-**syahl**), space helmet, 23

el casete (el kah-**say**-tay), cassette tape, 2

el castillo (el kahs-**tee**-yo), castle, 25

la catarata (lah kah-tah-**rah**-tah), waterfall, 32

catorce (kah-**tor**-say), fourteen, 31

cavar (kah-**bar**), dig, 27

la caverna (lah kah-**ber**-nah), cave, 24

los cavernícolas (los kah-ber-**nee**-ko-lahs), cave dwellers, 24

la caza (lah **kah**-sah), hunt, 26

el cazador (el kah-sah-**dor**), hunter, 24

las cebollas (lahs say-**bo**-yas), onions, 6

la cebra (lah **say**-brah), zebra, 20

la ceja (lah **say**-hah), eyebrow, 11

la cena (lah **say**-nah), dinner, 10

la cena congelada (lah **say**-nah kon-hay-**lah**-dah), frozen dinner, 6

el cepillo (el say-**pee**-yo), brush, 12

el cepillo de dientes (el say-**pee**-yo day **dyen**-tes), toothbrush, 11

cerca de (**ser**-kah day), near, 26

la cerca (lah **ser**-kah), fence, 9

el cerdo (el **ser**-do), pig, 9

el cereal (el say-ray-**ahl**), cereal, 6

las cerezas (lahs say-**ray**-sahs), cherries, 6

cero (**say**-ro), zero, 31

cerrado (say-**rrah**-do), closed, 26

la cerradura (lah say-rrah-**doo**-rah), lock, 13

cerrar (say-**rrar**), close, 27

el ciclismo (el see-**klees**-mo), cycling, 18

el cielo (el **syay**-lo), sky, 9

cien (syen), one hundred, 31

cien mil (syen **meel**), one hundred thousand, 31

el científico (el syen-**tee**-fee-ko), scientist, 23

el ciervo (el **syer**-bo), deer, 20

el cilindro (el see-**leen**-dro), cylinder, 30

los címbalos (los **seem**-bah-los), cymbals, 19

cinco (**seen**-ko), five, 31

cincuenta (seen-**kwen**-tah), fifty, 31

cincuenta y cinco (seen-**kwen**-tah ee **seen**-ko), fifty-five, 31

cincuenta y cuatro (seen-**kwen**-tah ee **kwah**-tro), fifty-four, 31

cincuenta y dos (seen-**kwen**-tah ee **dos**), fifty-two, 31

cincuenta y nueve (seen-**kwen**-tah ee **nway**-bay), fifty-nine, 31

cincuenta y ocho (seen-**kwen**-tah ee o-cho), fifty-eight, 31

cincuenta y seis (seen-**kwen**-tah ee **says**), fifty-six, 31

cincuenta y siete (seen-**kwen**-tah ee **syay**-tay), fifty-seven, 31

cincuenta y tres (seen-**kwen**-tah ee **tres**), fifty-three, 31

cincuenta y uno (seen-**kwen**-tah ee **oo**-no), fifty-one, 31

el cine (el **see**-nay), movie theater, 8

la cinta (lah **seen**-tah), packing tape, 13

la cinta adhesiva (lah **seen**-tah ad-ay-**see**-ba), cellophane tape, 1

la cinta de goma (lah **seen**-tah day **go**-mah), rubber band, 13

la cinta para medir (lah **seen**-tah pah-rah may-**deer**), tape measure, 3

el cinturón (el seen-too-**ron**), belt, 7

el cinturón de seguridad (el seen-too-ron day say-goo-ree-**dad**), seat belt, 14

el circo (el **seer**-ko), circus, 21

el círculo (el **seer**-koo-lo), circle, 30

el cisne (el **sees**-nay), swan, 20

la ciudad (lah-syoo-**dahd**), city, 8

el clarinete (el klah-ree-**nay**-tay), clarinet, 19

claro (**klah**-ro), light, 26

el clavo (el **klah**-bo), nail, 3

la cocina (lah ko-**see**-nah), kitchen, 2, 3

cocinar (ko-see-**nar**), cook, 27

el cocinero (el ko-see-**nay**-ro), cook, 15

el coche (el **ko**-chay), car, 16

el coche de bomberos (el **ko**-chay day bom-**bay**-ros), fire engine, 16

el coche de carreras (el **ko**-chay day kah-**rray**-rahs), race car, 14

el coche de policía (el **ko**-chay day po-lee-**see**-ah), police car, 16

el cochecito (el ko-chay-**see**-to), baby carriage, 16

el cochecito de niño (el ko-chay-**see**-to day **nee**-nyo), stroller, 16

el cochinillo (el ko-chee-**nee**-yo), piglet, 9

el código postal (el **ko**-dee-go pos-**tahl**), zip code, 13

el codo (el **ko**-do), elbow, 11

el cohete (el ko-**ay**-tay), rocket, 23

la col (lah kol), cabbage, 6

la cola (lah **ko**-lah), glue, 1; tail, 20

la cola de caballo (lah **ko**-lah day kah-**bah**-yo), ponytail, 12

el colgadero (el kol-gah-**day**-ro), hanger, 2

la colina (lah ko-**lee**-nah), hill, 9

el colmillo (el kol-**mee**-yo), tusk, 24

los colores (los co-**lo**-res), colors, 28

los columpios (los ko-**loom**-pyos), swings, 8

el collar (el ko-**yar**), necklace, 7

el comedor (el ko-may-**dor**), dining room, 2

comer (ko-**mer**), eat, 27

el cometa (el ko-**may**-tah), comet, 23

la cometa (lah ko-**may**-tah), kite, 5

la comida (lah ko-**mee**-dah), food, 6

las comidas (lahs ko-**mee**-dahs), meals, 10

el compartimiento de flete (el kom-par-tee-myen-to day **flay**-tay), cargo bay, 23

el compás (el kom-**pahs**), compass, 1

comprar (kom-**prar**), buy, 27

la computadora (lah kom-poo-tah-**do**-rah), computer, 23

la comunidad (lah co-moo-nee-**dahd**), community, 15

el Concorde (el kon-**kor**-day), Concorde, 17

la concha de mar (lah **kon**-chah day mar), seashell, 22

la conductora de autobús (lah kon-dook-to-rah day ow-to-**boos**), bus driver, 15

el conejo (el ko-**nay**-ho), rabbit, 9

el congelador (el kon-hay-lah-**dor**), freezer, 3

el cono (el **ko**-no), cone, 30

la constelación (lah kons-tay-lah-**syon**), constellation, 23

la contraseña de equipaje (lah kon-trah-**say**-nyah day ay-kee-**pah**-hay), baggage claim, 17

la controladora de tráfico (lah kon-tro-lah-**do**-rah day **trah**-fee-ko), air-traffic controller, 17

la copiloto (lah ko-pee-**lo**-to), copilot, 17

el copo de nieve (el **ko**-po day **nye**-bay), snowflake, 5

el coral (el ko-**rahl**), coral, 22

la corbata (lah kor-**bah**-tah), tie, 7

el cordel (el kor-**del**), string, 13

el cordero (el kor-**day**-ro), lamb, 9

el cordón (el kor-**don**), shoelace, 7

el corno francés (el **kor**-no frahn-**ses**), French horn, 19

la corona (lah ko-**ro**-nah), crown, 25

el correo (el ko-**rray**-o), post office, 13

correr (ko-**rrer**), run, 27

el correr (el ko-**rrer**), running, 18

la cortadora de grama (lah kor-tah-**do**-rah day **grah**-mah), lawn mower, 5

cortar, (kor-**tar**), cut, 27

el cortaúñas (el kor-tah-**oo**-nyahs), nail clippers, 12

el corte de cepillo (el **kor**-tay day say-**pee**-yo), crew cut, 12

las cortinas (lahs kor-**tee**-nahs), curtains, 2

corto (**kor**-to), short, 12, 26

la cosecha (lah ko-**say**-chah), crop, 24

la cota de mallas (lah **ko**-tah day **mah**-yahs), chain mail, 25

el cráter (el **krah**-ter), crater, 23

la crema (lah **kray**-mah), cream, 10

la crema de afeitar (lah **kray**-mah day ah-fay-**tar**), shaving cream, 12

la cremallera (lah kray-mah-**yay**-rah), zipper, 7

el creyón (el kray-**yon**), crayon, 1

el cruce de peatones (el **kroo**-say day pay-ah-**to**-nes), crosswalk, 16

el crucero (el kroo-**say**-ro), cruise ship, 16

el cuaderno (el kwah-**der**-no), notebook, notepad, 1, 13

el cuadrado (el kwah-**drah**-do), square, 30

el cuadro (el **kwah**-dro), picture, 1

el cuadro de jardín (el **kwah**-dro day har-**deen**), flowerbed, 5

cuarenta (kwah-**ren**-tah), forty, 31

cuarenta y cinco (kwah-**ren**-tah ee **seen**-ko), forty-five, 31

cuarenta y cuatro (kwah-**ren**-tah ee **kwah**-tro), forty-four, 31

cuarenta y dos (kwah-**ren**-tah ee **dos**), forty-two, 31

cuarenta y nueve (kwah-**ren**-tah ee **nway**-bay), forty-nine, 31

cuarenta y ocho (kwah-**ren**-tah ee o-cho), forty-eight, 31

cuarenta y seis (kwah-**ren**-tah ee **says**), forty-six, 31

cuarenta y siete (kwah-**ren**-tah ee **syay**-tay), forty-seven, 31

cuarenta y tres (kwah-**ren**-tah ee **tres**), forty-three, 31

cuarenta y uno (kwah-**ren**-tah ee **oo**-no), forty-one, 31

cuarto (**kwar**-to), fourth, 31

el cuarto de auxilio (el **kwar**-to day ow-**gsee**-lyo), utility room, 3

el cuarto de baño (el **kwar**-to day **bah**-nyo), bathroom, 2

cuatro (**kwah**-tro), four, 31

el cubo (el **koo**-bo), cube, 30

los cubos (los **koo**-bos), blocks, 4

los cubos de hielo (los **koo**-bos day **yay**-lo), ice cubes, 3

la cuchara (lah koo-**chah**-rah), spoon, 10

el cuchillo (el koo-**chee**-yo), knife, 10

el cuello (el **kway**-yo), collar, 7

la cuerda (lah **kwer**-dah), rope, string, 4, 19, 21

la cuerda de brincar (lah **kwer**-dah day breen-**kar**), jump rope, 4

la cuerda floja (lah **kwer**-dah **flo**-hah), tightrope, 21
las cuerdas (lahs **kwer**-dahs), strings, 19
los cuernos (los **kwer**-nos), horns, 9, 20
el cuero (el **kway**-ro), leather, 24
la cuna (lah **koo**-nah), cradle, 4
el chaleco de plumón (el chah-**lay**-ko day ploo-**mon**), down vest, 7
el champú (el chahm-**poo**), shampoo, 12
la chaqueta (lah chah-**kay**-tah), jacket, 7
el charco (el **char**-ko), puddle, 5
el cheque (el **chay**-kay), check, 13
la chimenea (lah chee-may-**nay**-ah), chimney, fireplace, 2; smokestack, 8
el chivato (el chee-**bah**-to), kid, 9
el chocolate (el cho-ko-**lah**-tay), chocolate, 6

los dados (los **dah**-dos), dice, 4
dar (dar), give, 27
debajo de (day-**bah**-ho day), under, 26
décimo (**day**-see-mo), tenth, 31
el decorado (el day-ko-**rah**-do), scenery, 19
el dedo (el **day**-do), finger, 11; **(del pie)**, toe, 11
de ficción (day feek-**syon**), make-believe, 25
el delantal (el day-lan-**tal**), apron, 3
el delfín (el del-**feen**), dolphin, 22
delgado (del-**gah**-do), thin, 26
el dentista (el den-**tees**-tah), dentist, 11
dentro de (**den**-tro day), inside, 26
los deportes (los day-**por**-tes), sports, 18
derecho (day-**ray**-cho), right, 26
el desayuno (el day-sah-**yoo**-no), breakfast, 10
el desfile del circo (el des-**fee**-lay del **seer**-ko), circus parade, 21
el desierto (el day-**syer**-to), desert, 32
despacio (des-**pah**-syo), slow, 26
el despertador (el des-per-tah-**dor**), alarm clock, 2
el destornillador (el des-tor-nee-yah-**dor**), screwdriver, 3
el desván (el des-**bahn**), attic, 4
el detergente (el day-ter-**hen**-tay), laundry detergent, 3
detrás de (day-**trahs** day), behind, 26
dibujar (dee-boo-**har**), draw, 27
el dibujo de caverna (el dee-**boo**-ho day kah-**ber**-nah), cave drawing, 24
diecinueve (dyay-see-**nway**-bay), nineteen, 31
dieciocho (dyay-see-**o**-cho), eighteen, 31
dieciséis (dyay-see-**says**), sixteen, 31
diecisiete (dyay-see-**syay**-tay), seventeen, 31
el diente (el **dyen**-tay), tooth, 11
diez (dyes), ten, 31
diez mil (dyes **meel**), ten thousand, 31
difícil (dee-**fee**-seel), difficult, 26
el dinero (el dee-**nay**-ro), money, 6
el dinosaurio (el dee-no-**sow**-ryo), dinosaur, 24
la dirección (lah dee-rek-**syon**), address, 13
el director (el dee-rek-**tor**), conductor, 19
el dirigible (el dee-ree-**hee**-blay), blimp, 16
el disc jockey (el deesk **yo**-kay), disc jockey, 15
el disco (el **dees**-ko), record, 2
el disco compacto (el **dees**-ko kom-**pahk**-to), compact disc, 2
la diseñadora de modas (lah dee-say-nyah-**do**-rah day **mo**-dahs), fashion designer, 15
el disfraz (el dees-**frahs**), costume, 19
doce (**do**-say), twelve, 31
el domador de fieras (el do-mah-**dor** day **fyay**-rahs), lion tamer, 21
dorado (do-**rah**-do), gold, 28

dormir (dor-**meer**), sleep, 27
el dormitorio (el dor-mee-**to**-ryo), bedroom, 2
dos (dos), two, 31
el dragón (el drah-**gon**), dragon, 25
la ducha (lah **doo**-chah), shower, 2
el duende (el **dwen**-day), elf, 25
los dulces (los **dool**-ses), candy, 6
el durazno (el doo-**rahs**-no), peach, 6
duro (**doo**-ro), hard, 26

el ecuador (el ay-kwah-**dor**), equator, 32
el edificio (el ay-dee-**fee**-syo), building, 8
el edificio de apartamentos (el ay-dee-**fee**-syo day ah-par-tah-**men**-tos), apartment building, 8
el electricista (el ay-lek-tree-**sees**-tah), electrician, 15
el elefante (el ay-lay-**fahn**-tay), elephant, 20, 21
el embotellamiento de tráfico (el em-bo-tay-yah-**myen**-to day **trah**-fee-ko), traffic jam, 8
la empanada (lah em-pah-**nah**-dah), pie, 6
el empleado postal (el em-play-**ah**-do pos-**tahl**), postal worker, 13
empujar (em-poo-**har**), push, 27
encendido (en-sen-**dee**-do), on, 26
encima de (en-**see**-mah day), on top of, 26
encontrar (en-kon-**trar**), find, 27
el enchufe (el en-**choo**-fay), electrical outlet, 3
el enfermero (el en-fer-**may**-ro), nurse, 11
enfrente de (en-**fren**-tay day), in front of, 26
la ensalada (lah en-sah-**lah**-dah), salad, 10
enseñar (en-say-**nyar**), teach, 27
las entradas (lahs en-**trah**-dahs), tickets, 21
entre (**en**-tray), between, 26
la equitación (lah ay-kee-tah-**syon**), horseback riding, 18
el erizo marino (el ay-**ree**-so mah-**ree**-no), sea urchin, 22
la escalera (lah es-kah-**lay**-rah), ladder, 23; stairs, 2
la escalera de cuerda (lah es-kah-**lay**-rah day **kwer**-dah), rope ladder, 21
la escalera de incendios (lah es-kah-**lay**-rah day een-**sen**-dyos), fire escape, 8
la escalera mecánica (lah es-kah-**lay**-rah may-**kah**-nee-kah), escalator, 17
las escamas (lahs es-**kah**-mahs), scales, 22
la escayola (lah es-kah-**yo**-lah), cast, 11
el escenario (el es-say-**nah**-ryo), stage, 19
la escoba (lah es-**ko**-bah), broom, 3
escribir (es-kree-**beer**), write, 27
el escritorio (el es-kree-**to**-ryo), teacher's desk, 1
escuchar (es-koo-**char**), listen (to), 27
el escudero (el es-koo-**day**-ro), squire, 25
el escudo (el es-**koo**-do), shield, 25
la escuela (lah es-**kway**-lah), school, 8
la esfera (lah es-**fay**-rah), sphere, 30
el esmalte (el es-**mahl**-tay), nail polish, 12
el esmoquin (el es-**mo**-keen), tuxedo, 4
el esnórquel (el es-**nor**-kel), snorkel, 22
el espacio (el es-**pah**-syo), space, 23
la espada (lah es-**pah**-dah), sword, 25
la espalda (lah es-**pahl**-dah), back, 11
la espátula (lah es-**pah**-too-lah), spatula, 3
el espectáculo (el es-pek-**tah**-koo-lo), talent show, 19
el espejo (el es-**pay**-ho), mirror, 2
el espejo retrovisor (el es-**pay**-ho ray-tro-bee-**sor**), rearview mirror, 14
esperar (es-pay-**rar**), wait, 27
¡Espere! (es-**pay**-ray), Wait!, 16
las espinacas (lahs es-pee-**nah**-kahs), spinach, 6

la esponja (lah es-**pon**-hah), sponge, 3
la espuma (lah es-**poo**-mah), suds, 12
la espuma de pelo (lah es-**poo**-mah day **pay**-lo), mousse, 12
el esqueleto (el es-kay-**lay**-to), skeleton, 24
el esquí alpino (el es-**kee** ahl-**pee**-no), downhill skiing, 18
el esquí nórdico (el es-**kee** nor-**dee**-ko), cross-country skiing, 18
esquiar (es-**kyar**), ski, 27
la esquina (lah es-**kee**-nah), corner, 8
los esquís (los es-**kees**), skis, 18
el establo (el es-**tah**-blo), stable, 25
las estaciones (lahs es-tah-**syo**-nes), seasons, 5
la estación de bomberos (lah es-tah-**syon** day bom-**bay**-ros), fire station, 8
la estación de policía (lah es-tah-**syon** day po-lee-**see**-ah), police station, 8
la estación del tren (lah es-tah-**syon** del tren), train station, 8
la estación espacial (lah es-tah-**syon** es-pah-**syahl**), space station, 23
el estandarte (el es-tahn-**dar**-tay), banner, 25
el estanque (el es-**tahn**-kay), pond, 9
el estante (el es-**tahn**-tay), shelf, 2
la estantería (lah es-tahn-tay-**ree**-ah), bookcase, 1
la estatua (lah es-**tah**-twah), statue, 8
este (**es**-tay), east, 32
el estetoscopio (el es-tay-to-**sko**-pyo), stethoscope, 11
el estornudo (el es-tor-**noo**-do), sneeze, 11
estrecho (es-**tray**-cho), narrow, 26
la estrella de mar (lah es-**tray**-yah day mar), starfish, 22
las estrellas (lahs es-**tray**-yahs), stars, 23
el estribo (el es-**tree**-bo), stirrup, 25
la estufa (lah es-**too**-fah), stove, 3
la etiqueta (lah ay-tee-**kay**-tah), label, 13
Europa (eoo-**ro**-pah), Europe, 32
la excursión (lah es-koor-**syon**), picnic, 9
el extraterrestre (el es-trah-tay-**rres**-tray), alien, 23

la fábrica (lah **fah**-bree-kah), factory, 8
fácil (**fah**-seel), easy, 26
la falda (lah **fahl**-dah), skirt, 7
la falla (lah **fah**-yah), fault, 32
la farmacéutica (lah far-mah-**seoo**-tee-kah), pharmacist, 15
la farmacia (lah far-**mah**-syah), drugstore, pharmacy, 8
el faro (el **fah**-ro), headlight, 14; lighthouse, 16
el farol (el fah-**rol**), handstand, 21
los faros de freno (los **fah**-ros day **fray**-no), brake lights, 14
feliz (fay-**lees**), happy, 26
los fideos (los fee-**day**-os), noodles, 10
la fiesta de cumpleaños (lah **fyes**-tah day koom-play-**ah**-nyos), birthday party, 10
la figura de nieve (lah fee-**goo**-rah day **nyay**-bay), snowman, 5
la firma (lah **feer**-mah), signature, 13
el flamenco (el flah-**men**-ko), flamingo, 20
la flauta (lah **flow**-tah), flute, 19
la flecha (lah **flay**-chah), arrow, 25
el flequillo (el flay-**kee**-yo), bangs, 12
la florera (lah flo-**ray**-rah), florist, 15
el florero (el flo-**ray**-ro), vase, 2
las flores (lahs **flo**-res), flowers, 5
la foca (lah **fo**-kah), seal, 20
las formas (lahs **for**-mahs), shapes, 30
los fósforos (los **fos**-fo-ros), matches, 5
el foso (el **fo**-so), moat, 25

el foso de la orquesta (el **fo**-so day lah or-**kes**-tah), orchestra pit, 19

la fotografía (lah fo-to-grah-**fee**-ah), photograph, 4

el fotógrafo (el fo-**to**-grah-fo), photographer, 15

la fragua (lah **frah**-gwah), forge, 25

las frambuesas (lahs frahm-**bway**-sahs), raspberries, 6

el fregadero (el fray-gah-**day**-ro), sink, 3

el freno manual (el **fray**-no mah-**nwahl**), hand brake, 14

los frenos (los **fray**-nos), braces, 11

la frente (lah **fren**-tay), forehead, 11

las fresas (lahs **fray**-sahs), strawberries, 6

frío (**free**-o), cold, 26

la fruta (lah **froo**-tah), fruit, 6

el fuego (el **fway**-go), fire, 24

la fuente (lah **fwen**-tay), fountain, 8

fuera de (**fwe**-rah day), outside, 26

el fútbol (el **foot**-bol), soccer, 18

el fútbol americano (el **foot**-bol ah-may-ree-**kah**-no), football, 18

el gabinete de medicina (el gah-bee-**nay**-tay day may-dee-**see**-nah), medicine cabinet, 2

las gafas protectoras (lahs **gah**-fahs pro-tek-**to**-rahs), goggles, 18

la galaxia (lah gah-**lah**-gsyah), galaxy, 23

las galletas (lahs gah-**yay**-tahs), crackers, 6

las galletas dulces (lahs gah-**yay**-tahs **dool**-ses), cookies, 6

la gallina (lah gah-**yee**-nah), hen, 9

el gallo (el **gah**-yo), rooster, 9

el gansarón (el gahn-sah-**ron**), gosling, 9

el ganso (el **gahn**-so), goose, 9

el garaje (el gah-**rah**-hay), garage, 14

las garras (lahs **gah**-rrahs), claws, 20

la gasolinera (lah gah-so-lee-**nay**-rah), gas station, 14

el gatito (el gah-**tee**-to), kitten, 9

el gato (el **gah**-to), cat, 9; jack, 14

la giba (lah **hee**-bah), hump, 20

el gigante (el hee-**gahn**-tay), giant, 25

la gimnasia (lah heem-**nah**-sya), gymnastics, 18

la gimnasta de la cuerda floja (lah heem-**nas**-tah day lah **kwer**-dah **flo**-hah), tightrope walker, 21

el glaciar (el glah-**syar**), glacier, 32

el globo (el **glo**-bo), balloon, 21; hot-air balloon, 16

el globo terráqueo (el **glo**-bo tay-**rrah**-kay-o), globe, 1

el golf (el golf), golf, 18

el golfo (el **gol** fo), gulf, 32

la goma de borrar (lah **go**-mah day bo-**rrar**), eraser (pencil), 1

gordo (**gor**-do), fat, 26

el gorila (el go-**ree**-lah), gorilla, 20

el gorro (el **go**-rro), cap, 7

la gota de lluvia (lah **go**-tah day **yoo**-byah), raindrop, 5

la grabadora (lah grah-bah-**do**-rah), cassette player, 2

grande (**grahn**-day), large, 26

el granero (el grah-**nay**-ro), barn, 9

la granja (lah **grahn**-hah), farm, 9

el granjero (el grahn-**hay**-ro), farmer, 9

la grapadora (lah grah-pah-**do**-rah), stapler, 1

las grapas (lahs **grah**-pahs), staples, 1

el grifo (el **gree**-fo), faucet, 3

gris (grees), gray, 28

la grúa (lah **groo**-ah), crane, 8; tow truck, 14

los guantes (los **gwahn**-tes), gloves, 7

los guantes de boxeo (los **gwahn**-tes day bo-**gsay**-o), boxing gloves, 18

el guardalodo (el gwar-dah-**lo**-do), fender, 14

el guardia de seguridad (el **gwar**-dyah day say-goo-ree-**dahd**), security guard, 13

el guardián de zoológico (el gwar-**dyahn** day so-o-**lo**-hee-ko), zookeeper, 20

la guía (lah **gee**-ah), tour guide, 15

el guión (el gee-**on**), script, 19

los guisantes (los gee-**sahn**-tes), peas, 6

la guitarra (lah gee-**tah**-rrah), guitar, 19

el gusano (el goo-**sah**-no), worm, 5

hablar (ah-**blar**), talk, 27

hacer juegos malabares (ah-**ser hway**-gos mah-lah-**bah**-res), juggle, 27

el hacha (el **ah**-chah), ax, 25

el hada (el **ah**-dah), fairy, 25

la hamaca (lah ah-**mah**-kah), hammock, 5

la hamburguesa (lah ahm-boor-**gay**-sah), hamburger, 10

el hangar (el ahn-**gar**), hangar, 17

la harina (lah ah-**ree**-nah), flour, 3

la hebilla (lah ay-**bee**-yah), buckle, 7

el helado (el ay-**lah**-do), ice cream, 10

el helecho (el ay-**lay**-cho), fern, 24

la hélice (lah **ay**-lee-say), propeller, 17

el helicóptero (el ay-lee-**kop**-tay-ro), helicopter, 16

la hermana (lah er-**mah**-nah), sister, 29

el hermano (el er-**mah**-no), brother, 29

la herradura (lah ay-rrah-**doo**-rah), horseshoe, 25

el herrero (el ay-**rray**-ro), blacksmith, 25

el hielo (el **ye**-lo), ice, 5

la hierba (lah **yer**-bah), grass, 9

la higienista dental (lah ee-hye-**nees**-tah den-**tahl**), dental hygienist, 11

la hija (lah **ee**-hah), daughter, 29

el hijo (el **ee**-ho), son, 29

el hilado (el ee-**lah**-do), yarn, 4

el hilo de pescar (el **ee**-lo day pes-**kar**), fishing line, 22

el hipocampo (el ee-po-**kahm**-po), sea horse, 22

el hipopótamo (el ee-po-**po**-tah-mo), hippopotamus, 20

la historia de la humanidad (lah ees-**to**-ryah day lah oo-mah-nee-**dahd**), human history, 24

el hockey (el **ho**-kay), hockey, 18

la hoja (lah **o**-hah), leaf, 5

el hombre (el **om**-bray), man, 9

el hombro (el **om**-bro), shoulder, 11

el hongo (el **on**-go), mushroom, 10

la hormiga (lah or-**mee**-gah), ant, 9

el horno (el **or**-no), kiln, 24; oven, 3

el horno de microondas (el **or**-no day mee-kro-**on**-dahs), microwave oven, 3

la hortaliza (lah or-tah-**lee**-sah), vegetable garden, 5

el hospital (el os-pee-**tahl**), hospital, 8

el hotel (el o-**tel**), hotel, 8

la hucha (lah **oo**-chah), piggy bank, 13

la huella del pie (lah **we**-yah del **pyay**), footprint, 23

el hueso (el **way**-so), bone, 24

los huevos (los **way**-bos), eggs, 6

el humo (el **oo**-mo), smoke, 9

la iglesia (lah ee-**glay**-syah), church, 8

el imán (el ee-**mahn**), magnet, 4

el impermeable (el eem-per-may-**ah**-blay), raincoat, 7

el indicador de metales (el een-dee-kah-**dor** day may-**tah**-les), metal detector, 17

el inodoro (el ee-no-**do**-ro), toilet, 2

el insecto (el een-**sek**-to), insect, 24

la intersección (lah een-ter-sek-**syon**), intersection, 16

el invierno (el een-**byer**-no), winter, 5

ir (eer), go, 27

la isla (lah **ees**-lah), island, 32

izquierdo (ees-**kyer**-do), left, 26

el jabón (el hah-**bon**), soap, 6

el jaguar (el hah-**gwar**), jaguar, 20

el jamón (el hah-**mon**), ham, 10

el jardín zoológico (el har-**deen** so-o-**lo**-hee-ko), zoo, 20

el jardinero (el har-dee-**nay**-ro), gardener, 15

la jaula (lah **how**-lah), cage, 21

el jeep (el yeep), jeep, 16

la jinete (lah hee-**nay**-tay), bareback rider, 21

la jirafa (lah hee-**rah**-fah), giraffe, 20

el jogging (el **yo**-geen), jogging, 18

la joya (lah **ho**-yah), jewel, 22

el joyero (el ho-**yay**-ro), jeweler, 15

las judías verdes (lahs hoo-**dee**-ahs **ber**-des), green beans, 6

el juego (el **hway**-go), game, 4

el juego de auriculares (el **hway**-go day ow-ree-koo-**lah**-res), headset, 17

el juego de damas (el **hway**-go day **dah**-mahs), checkers, 4

la juez (el **hwes**), judge, 15

jugar (hoo-**gar**), play (a game), 27

jugar a los bolos (hoo-**gar** ah los **bo**-los), bowling, 18

el jugo (el **hoo**-go), fruit juice, 6

la juguetería (lah hoo-gay-tay-**ree**-ah), toy store, 8

los juguetes (los hoo-**gay**-tes), toys, 4

los labios (los **lah**-byos), lips, 11

el laboratorio (el lah-bo-rah-**to**-ryo), laboratory, 23

la laca (lah **lah**-kah), hair spray, 12

al lado de (ahl **lah**-do day), next to, 26

el ladrillo (el lah-**dree**-yo), brick, 3

el lagarto (el lah-**gar**-to), lizard, 20

el lago (el **lah**-go), lake, 32

la lámpara (lah **lahm**-pah-rah), lamp, 2

la lámpara flash (lah **lahm**-pah-rah flahsh), flashbulb, 21

la lancha (lah **lahn**-chah), motorboat, 16

la langosta (lah lahn-**gos**-tah), lobster, 22

la lanza (lah **lahn**-sah), lance, spear, 24, 25

los lápices de color (los **lah**-pee-ses day ko-**lor**), colored pencils, 1

el lápiz (el **lah**-pees), pencil, 1

el lápiz de labios (el **lah**-pees day **lah**-byos), lipstick, 12

largo (**lar**-go), long, 12, 26

la lata (lah **lah**-tah), can, 6

el látigo (el **lah**-tee-go), whip, 21

el lavado de coches (el lah-**bah**-do day **ko**-ches), car wash, 14

la lavadora (lah lah-bah-**do**-rah), washing machine, 3

el lavaplatos (el lah-bah-**plah**-tos), dishwasher, 3

lavarse (lah-**bar**-say), wash oneself, 27

el lazo (el **lah**-so), bow, 11

la leche (lah **lay**-chay), milk, 6

la lechuga (lah lay-**choo**-gah), lettuce, 6

la lechuza (lah lay-**choo**-sah), owl, 20

leer (lay-**er**), read, 27

las legumbres (las lay-**goom**-bres), vegetables, 6

lejos de (**lay**-hos day), far, 26

la lengua (lah **len**-gwah), tongue, 11
el león (el lay-**on**), lion, 20, 21
el leopardo (el lay-o-**par**-do), leopard, 20
el letrero (el lay-**tray**-ro), sign, 6
el levantamiento de pesos (el lay-bahn-tah-**myen**-to day **pay**-sos), weight lifting, 18
la librería (lah lee-bray-**ree**-ah), bookstore, 8
el librero (el lee-**bray**-ro), bookseller, 15
el libro (el **lee**-bro), book, 1
el libro de colorear (el **lee**-bro day ko-lo-ray-**ar**), coloring book, 4
los libros de cómicos (los **lee**-bros day **ko**-mee-kos), comic books, 4
ligero (lee-**hay**-ro), light, 26
la lima (lah **lee**-mah), file, nail file, 3, 12
el limón (el lee-**mon**), lemon, 6
el limón verde (el lee-**mon ber**-day), lime, 6
los limpiaparabrisas (los leem-pya-pah-rah-**bree**-sahs), windshield wipers, 14
limpio (**leem**-pyo), clean, 26
la linterna eléctrica (lah leen-**ter**-nah ay-**lek**-tree-kah), flashlight, 3
liso (**lee**-so), straight, 12
el lobo (el **lo**-bo), wolf, 20
el lodo (el **lo**-do), mud, 5
el loro (el **lo**-ro), parrot, 20
la lucha libre (lah **loo**-chah **lee**-bray), wrestling, 18
la luna (lah **loo**-nah), moon, 23
la llanta (lah **yahn**-tah), tire, 14
la llanta reventada (lah **yahn**-tah ray-ben-**tah**-dah), flat tire, 14
la llanura (lah yah-**noo**-rah), plain, 32
la llave (lah **yah**-bay), key, 13
la llave de tuercas (lah **yah**-bay day **twer**-kahs), wrench, 3
lleno (**yay**-no), full, 26
llevar (yay-**bar**), carry, 27
llorar (yo-**rar**), cry, 27
la lluvia (lah **yoo**-byah), rain, 5
la lluvia meteórica (lah **yoo**-byah may-tay-o-ree-kah), meteor shower, 23

la madera (lah mah-**day**-rah), wood, 3
la madre (lah **mah**-dray), mother, 29
la maestra (lah mah-**es**-trah), teacher (female), 1
el maestro (el mah-**es**-tro), teacher (male), 1
el maestro de ceremonias (el mah-**es**-tro day say-ray-**mo**-nyahs), ringmaster, 21
el mago (el **mah**-go), magician, 21
el maíz (el mah-**ees**), corn, 24
el malabarista (el mah-lah-bah-**rees**-tah), juggler, 21
la maleta (lah mah-**lay**-tah), suitcase, 17
la maleta para vestidos y trajes (lah mah-**lay**-tah **pah**-rah bes-**tee**-dos ee **trah**-hes), garment bag, 17
malo (**mah**-lo), bad, 26
la malla (lah **mah**-yah), leotard, 19
la mamá (lah mah-**mah**), mom, 29
el mamut (el mah-**moot**), mammoth, 24
las manchas (lahs **mahn**-chas), spots, 20
la manecilla (lah mah-nay-**see**-yah), hand (of a clock), 1
manejar (mah-nay-**har**), drive, 27
la manga (lah **mahn**-gah), sleeve, 7
la manga de aire (lah **mahn**-gah day **igh**-ray), air hose, 14
la manguera de jardín (lah mahn-**gay**-rah day har-**deen**), garden hose, 5

la manicura (lah mah-nee-**koo**-rah), manicurist, 12
la manilla (lah mah-**nee**-yah), door handle, 14
el manillar (el mah-nee-**yar**), handlebars, 14
la mano (lah **mah**-no), hand, 11
las manoplas (lahs mah-**no**-plahs), mittens, 7
la manta (lah **mahn**-tah), blanket, 2
el mantel (el mahn-**tel**), tablecloth, 10
la mantequilla (lah mahn-tay-**kee**-yah), butter, 6
el manto de hielo (el **mahn**-to day **yay**-lo), icecap, 32
la manzana (lah mahn-**sah**-nah), apple, 6
la manzana de caramelo (lah mahn-**sah**-nah day kah-rah-**may**-lo), caramel apple, 21
el mapa (el **mah**-pah), map, 1
un mapamundi (oon mah-pah-**moon**-dee), map of the world, 32
el maquillaje (el mah-kee-**yah**-hay), makeup, 19
la máquina barredora de nieve (lah **mah**-kee-nah bah-rray-**do**-rah day **nyay**-bay), snowplow, 5
la máquina de coser (lah **mah**-kee-nah day ko-**ser**), sewing machine, 19
la máquina de escribir (lah **mah**-kee-nah day es-kree-**beer**), typewriter, 13
el mar (el mar), ocean, sea, 22, 32
el marco (el **mar**-ko), picture frame, 4
el marinero (el mah-ree-**nay**-ro), sailor, 15
la mariposa (lah mah-ree-**po**-sah), butterfly, 5
el martillo (el mar-**tee**-yo), hammer, 3
la máscara (lah **mahs**-kah-rah), mask, 19, 22
el matamoscas (el mah-tah-**mos**-kahs), fly swatter, 5
el matasellos (el mah-tah-**say**-yos), postmark, 13
el mecánico (el may-**kah**-nee-ko), mechanic, 14
la mecedora (lah may-say-**do**-rah), rocking chair, 2, 4
la medalla (lah may-**dah**-yah), medal, 18
mediano (may-**dyah**-no), medium, 26
la médica (lah **may**-dee-kah), doctor, 11
la medicina (lah may-dee-**see**-nah), medicine, 11
la medusa (lah may-**doo**-sah), jellyfish, 22
la mejilla (lah may-**hee**-yah), cheek, 11
la melena (lah may-**lay**-nah), mane, 20
el melón (el may-**lon**), melon, 6
el menú (el may-**noo**), menu, 10
la mermelada (lah mer-may-**lah**-dah), jam, 10
la mesa (lah **may**-sah), table, 3
la mesa de noche (lah **may**-sah day **no**-chay), night table, 2
la mesa de planchar (lah **may**-sah day plahn-**char**), ironing board, 3
el meteorólogo (el may-tay-o-**ro**-lo-go), weather forecaster, 15
el mezclador de cemento (el mes-klah-**dor** day say-**men**-to), cement mixer, 16
el micrófono (el mee-**kro**-fo-no), microphone, 19
el microscopio (el mee-kros-**ko**-pyo), microscope, 23
mil (meel), one thousand, 31
mil millones (meel mee-**yo**-nes), one billion, 31
un millón (oon mee-**yon**), one million, 31
mirar (mee-**rar**), watch, 27
la mitad (lah mee-**tahd**), one-half, 31
la mochila (lah mo-**chee**-lah), backpack, 7
la modelo (lah mo-**day**-lo), model, 15
mojado (mo-**hah**-do), wet, 26
la moneda (lah mo-**nay**-dah), coin, 13
el mono (el **mo**-no), coveralls, 14; monkey, 20
el monociclo (el mo-no-**see**-klo), unicycle, 21
las montañas (lahs mon-**tah**-nyahs), mountains, 32
montar en bicicleta (mon-**tar** en bee-see-**klay**-tah), ride a bicycle, 27

el moño (el **mo**-nyo), bun, 12
morado (mo-**rah**-do), purple, 28
moreno (mo-**ray**-no), brown, 12
la morsa (lah **mor**-sah), walrus, 20
la mosca (lah **mos**-kah), fly, 5
la mostaza (lah mos-**tah**-sah), mustard, 10
el mostrador (el mos-trah-**dor**), counter, 3
el mostrador de boletos (el mos-trah-**dor** day bo-**lay**-tos), ticket counter, 17
la motocicleta (lah mo-to-see-**klay**-tah), motorcycle, 16
el motor (el mo-**tor**), engine, 14, 17
el mozo (el **mo**-so), porter, 17
el mozo de equipaje (el **mo**-so day ay-kee-**pah**-hay), baggage handler, 17
el muelle (el **mway**-yay), dock, 16
la mujer (lah moo-**her**), woman, 9
la muleta (lah moo-**lay**-tah), crutch, 11
la muñeca (lah moo-**nyay**-kah), doll, 4
el murciélago (el moor-**syay**-lah-go), bat, 25
el museo (el moo-**say**-o), museum, 8
la música (lah **moo**-see-kah), sheet music, 19

nadar (nah-**dar**), swim, 27
los naipes (los **nigh**-pes), cards, 4
la naranja (lah nah-**ran**-hah), orange, 6
la nariz (lah nah-**rees**), nose, 11
la natación (lah nah-tah-**syon**), swimming, 18
el naufragio (el now-**frah**-hyo), shipwreck, 22
la navaja de afeitar (lah nah-**bah**-hah day ah-fay-**tar**), razor, 12
la navegación (lah nah-bay-gah-**syon**), sailing, 18
el navegante (el nah-bay-**gan**-tay), navigator, 17
la nebulosa (lah nay-boo-**lo**-sah), nebula, 23
negro (**nay**-gro), black, 12, 28
la nevera (lah nay-**bay**-rah), refrigerator, 3
el nido de pájaro (el **nee**-do day **pah**-hah-ro), bird's nest, 5
la niebla (lah **nye**-blah), fog, 5
la nieve (lah **nyay**-bay), snow, 5
la niña (lah **nee**-nyah), girl, 9
el niño (el **nee**-nyo), boy, 9
los niños (los **nee**-nyos), children, 19
la noche (lah **no**-chay), night, 21
nordeste (nor-**des**-tay), northeast, 32
noroeste (no-roes-**tay**), northwest, 32
norte (**nor**-tay), north, 32
noveno (no-**bay**-no), ninth, 31
noventa (no-**ben**-tah), ninety, 31
noventa y cinco (no-**ben**-tah ee **seen**-ko), ninety-five, 31
noventa y cuatro (no-**ben**-tah ee **kwah**-tro), ninety-four, 31
noventa y dos (no-**ben**-tah ee **dos**), ninety-two, 31
noventa y nueve (no-**ben**-tah ee **nway**-bay), ninety-nine, 31
noventa y ocho (no-**ben**-tah ee **o**-cho), ninety-eight, 31
noventa y seis (no-**ben**-tah ee **says**), ninety-six, 31
noventa y siete (no-**ben**-tah ee **syay**-tay), ninety-seven, 31
noventa y tres (no-**ben**-tah ee **tres**), ninety-three, 31
noventa y uno (no-**ben**-tah ee **oo**-no), ninety-one, 31
las nubes (lahs **noo**-bes), clouds, 5
el nudo (el **noo**-do), knot, 13
las nueces (lahs **nway**-ses), nuts, 6
nueve (**nway**-bay), nine, 31
nuevo (**nway**-bo), new, 26
los números (los **noo**-may-ros), numbers, 1, 31

los **números cardinales** (los **noo**-may-ros kar-dee-**nah**-les), cardinal numbers, 31
los **números ordinales** (los **noo**-may-ros or-dee-**nah**-les), ordinal numbers, 31

el **oasis** (el o-**ah**-sees), oasis, 32
el **obrero** (el o-**bray**-ro), construction worker, 15
el **Océano Atlántico** (el o-**say**-ah-no aht-**lahn**-tee-ko), Atlantic Ocean, 32
el **Océano Glacial Ártico** (el o-**say**-ah-no glah-**syahl** ar-tee-ko), Arctic Ocean, 32
el **Océano Índico** (el o-**say**-ah-no **een**-dee-ko), Indian Ocean, 32
el **Océano Pacífico** (el o-**say**-ah-no pah-**see**-fee-ko), Pacific Ocean, 32
el **octágono** (el ok-**tah**-go-no), octagon, 30
octavo (ok-**tah**-bo), eighth, 31
la **oculista** (lah o-koo-**lees**-tah), optician, 15
ochenta (o-**chen**-tah), eighty, 31
ochenta y cinco (o-**chen**-tah ee **seen**-ko), eighty-five, 31
ochenta y cuatro (o-**chen**-tah ee **kwah**-tro), eighty-four, 31
ochenta y dos (o-**chen**-tah ee **dos**), eighty-two, 31
ochenta y nueve (o-**chen**-tah ee **nway**-bay), eighty-nine, 31
ochenta y ocho (o-**chen**-tah ee **o**-cho), eighty-eight, 31
ochenta y seis (o-**chen**-tah ee **says**), eighty-six, 31
ochenta y siete (o-**chen**-tah ee **syay**-tay), eighty-seven, 31
ochenta y tres (o-**chen**-tah ee **tres**), eighty-three, 31
ochenta y uno (o-**chen**-tah ee **oo**-no), eighty-one, 31
ocho (o-cho), eight, 31
oeste (oes-tay), west, 32
la **oficina del dentista** (lah o-fee-**see**-nah del den-**tees**-tah), dentist's office, 11
la **oficina del médico** (lah o-fee-**see**-nah del **may**-dee-ko), doctor's office, 11
los **ojos** (los **o**-hos), eyes, 11
la **ola** (lah o-lah), wave, 22
once (**on**-say), eleven, 31
ondulado (on-doo-**lah**-do), wavy, 12
la **oreja** (lah o-**ray**-hah), ear, 11
las **orejeras** (lahs o-ray-**hay**-rahs), earmuffs, 7
el **oro** (el **o**-ro), gold, 22
la **orquesta** (lah or-**kes**-tah), orchestra, 19
oscuro (os-**koo**-ro), dark, 26
el **osito** (el o-**see**-to), teddy bear, 4
el **oso** (el **o**-so), bear, 20
el **oso polar** (el **o**-so po-**lar**), polar bear, 20
el **otoño** (el o-**to**-nyo), fall, 5
el **óvalo** (el **o**-bah-lo), oval, 30
la **oveja** (lah o-**bay**-hah), sheep, 9

el **paciente** (el pah-**syen**-tay), patient, 11
el **padre** (el **pah**-dray), father, 29
la **paja** (lah **pah**-hah), hay, 9; (drinking) straw, 10
el **pájaro** (el **pah**-hah-ro), bird, 5
la **pala** (lah **pah**-lah), shovel, 5
la **pala de basura** (lah **pah**-lah day bah-**soo**-rah), dustpan, 3
las **palabras** (lahs pah-**lah**-bras), words, 27
el **palo** (el **pah**-lo), club, stick, 24
el **palo de golf** (el **pah**-lo day golf), golf club, 18
el **palo de tienda** (el **pah**-lo day **tyen**-dah), tent pole, 21
las **palomitas** (lahs pah-lo-**mee**-tahs), popcorn, 21

el **pan** (el pahn), bread, 6
el **panda** (el **pahn**-dah), panda, 20
los **pantalones** (los pan-tah-**lo**-nes), pants, 7
los **pantalones cortos** (los pahn-tah-**lo**-nes **kor**-tos), shorts, 7
los **pantalones de entrenamiento** (los-pahn-tah-**lo**-nes day en-tray-nah-**myen**-to), sweatpants, 7
la **pantalla de radar** (lah pahn-**tah**-yah day rrah-**dar**), radar screen, 17
el **pañuelo** (el pah-**nyway**-lo), handkerchief, 7
el **papá** (el pah-**pah**), dad, 29
las **papas** (lahs **pah**-pahs), potatoes, 6
las **papas fritas** (lahs **pah**-pas **free**-tahs), french fries, 10
las **papas fritas a la inglesa** (lahs **pah**-pahs **free**-tahs ah lah een-**glay**-sah), potato chips, 6
el **papel** (el pah-**pel**), paper, 1
el **papel de lija** (el pah-**pel** day **lee**-hah), sandpaper, 3
el **papel higiénico** (el pah-**pel** ee-**hyay**-nee-ko), toilet paper, 2
la **papelera** (lah pah-pay-**lay**-rah), wastebasket, 1
el **paquete** (el pah-**kay**-tay), package, 13
el **parabrisas** (el pah-rah-**bree**-sahs), windshield, 14
el **paracaídas** (el pah-rah-kah-**ee**-dahs), parachute, 18
la **parada de autobús** (lah pah-**rah**-dah day ow-to-**boos**), bus stop, 16
la **parada de cabeza** (lah pah-**rah**-dah day kah-**bay**-sah), headstand, 21
el **paraguas** (el pah-**rah**-gwahs), umbrella, 4, 7
la **pared** (lah pah-**red**), wall, 2
el **parque** (el **par**-kay), park, 8
el **parquímetro** (el par-**kee**-may-tro), parking meter, 8
el **pasador** (el pah-sah-**dor**), barrette, 12
el **pasador de videos** (el pah-sah-**dor** day **bee**-day-os), videocassette player, 2
el **pasajero** (el pah-sah-**hay**-ro), passenger, 17
el **pasaporte** (el pah-sah-**por**-tay), passport, 17
la **pasta dentífrica** (lah **pas**-tah den-**tee**-free-kah), toothpaste, 11
la **pastelería** (lah pas-tay-lay-**ree**-ah), bakery, 8
la **pastilla** (lah pas-**tee**-yah), pill, 11
la **pastinaca** (lah pas-tee-**nah**-kah), stingray, 22
la **pata** (lah **pah**-tah), paw, 20
patear (pah-tay-**ar**), kick, 27
el **patinaje** (el pah-tee-**nah**-hay), skating, 18
patinar (pah-tee-**nar**), skate, 27
los **patines** (los pah-**tee**-nes), skates, 18
los **patines de ruedas** (los pah-**tee**-nes day **rrway**-das), roller skates, 16
el **patinete** (el pah-tee-**nay**-tay), scooter, 16
el **patio** (el **pah**-tyo), courtyard, yard, 25; deck, 5
el **patio de recreo** (el **pah**-tyo day ray-**kray**-o), playground, 8
el **patito** (el pah-**tee**-to), duckling, 9
el **pato** (el **pah**-to), duck, 9
el **pavo real** (el **pah**-bo ray-**al**), peacock, 20
la **payasa** (lah pah-**yah**-sah), clown, 21
las **pecas** (lahs **pay**-kahs), freckles, 12
el **pecho** (el **pay**-cho), chest, 11
el **pedal** (el pay-**dahl**), pedal, 14
el **pedernal** (el pay-der-**nahl**), flint, 24
la **pedicura** (lah pay-dee-**koo**-rah), pedicurist, 12
el **peine** (el **pay**-nay), comb, 12
la **película** (lah pay-**lee**-koo-lah), film, 21
pelirrojo (pay-lee-**rro**-ho), red, 12
el **pelo** (el **pay**-lo), hair, 12

la **pelota (de béisbol)** (lah pay-**lo**-tah), baseball, 18; **(de fútbol americano),** football, 18; **(de fútbol),** soccer ball, 18
la **peluca** (lah pay-**loo**-kah), wig, 19
la **peluquera** (lah pay-loo-**kay**-rah), hairstylist, 12
la **peluquería de caballeros y señoras** (lah pay-loo-kay-**ree**-ah day kah-bah-**yay**-ros ee say-**nyo**-rahs), barber shop, beauty salon, 12
la **península** (lah pay-**neen**-soo-lah), peninsula, 32
pensar (pen-**sar**), think, 27
pequeño (pay-**kay**-nyo), small, 26
el **percebe** (el per-**say**-bay), barnacle, 22
el **periódico** (el pay-**ryo**-dee-ko), newspaper, 8
el **periodista** (el pay-ryo-**dees**-tah), reporter, 15
las **persianas** (lahs per-**syah**-nahs), venetian blinds, 2
las **personas** (lahs-per-**so**-nahs), people, 15
el **perro** (el **pay**-rro), dog, 9
pesado (pay-**sah**-do), heavy, 26
la **pesca** (lah **pes**-kah), fishing, 24
el **pescado** (el pes-**kah**-do), fish, 10
el **pescador** (el pes-kah-**dor**), fisherman, 15
el **pétalo** (el **pay**-tah-lo), petal, 5
el **pez** (el pes), fish, 1
el **pez espada** (el pes es-**pah**-dah), swordfish, 22
el **piano** (el **pyah**-no), piano, 19
el **pico** (el **pee**-ko), beak, 20
el **pie** (el pyay), foot, 11
la **piedra** (lah **pyay**-drah), rock, 24
la **piedra de luna** (lah **pyay**-drah day **loo**-nah), moon rock, 23
la **piel** (lah **pyel**), fur, 24
la **pierna** (lah **pyer**-nah), leg, 11
el **pijama** (el pee-**hah**-mah), pajamas, 7
el **piloto** (el pee-**lo**-to), pilot, 17
la **pimienta** (lah pee-**myen**-tah), pepper, 10
la **piña** (lah **pee**-nyah), pineapple, 6
el **pincel** (el peen-**sel**), paintbrush, 1
el **pingüino** (el peen-**gwee**-no), penguin, 20
pintar (peen-**tar**), paint, 27
el **pintor** (el peen-**tor**), painter, 15
la **pintura** (lah peen-**too**-rah), paint, 1, 24
la **piscina** (lah pees-**see**-nah), swimming pool, 18
el **piso** (el **pee**-so), floor, 2
la **pista,** (lah **pees**-tah), runway, 17
la **pista de circo** (lah **pees**-tah day **seer**-ko), ring, 21
el **pito** (el **pee**-to), whistle, 4
la **pizarra** (lah pee-**sah**-rrah), chalkboard, 1
la **plancha** (lah **plahn**-chah), iron, 3
el **planeador** (el plah-nay-ah-**dor**), hang glider, 16
el **planeta** (el plah-**nay**-tah), planet, 23
la **planta** (lah **plahn**-tah), plant, 1
la **plata** (lah **plah**-tah), silver, 22
el **plátano** (el **plah**-tah-no), banana, 6
plateado (plah-tay-**ah**-do), silver, 28
el **platillo** (el plah-**tee**-yo), saucer, 10
el **platillo volante** (el plah-**tee**-yo bo-**lahn**-tay), spaceship, 23
el **plato** (el **plah**-to), plate, 10
los **platos** (los **plah**-tos), dishes, 3
la **playa** (lah **plah**-yah), beach, 8
la **plaza** (lah **plah**-sah), square, 8
el **plomero** (el plo-**may**-ro), plumber, 15
la **pluma** (lah **ploo**-mah), feather, 4
las **plumas** (lahs **ploo**-mahs), feathers, 20
el **policía** (el po-lee-**see**-ah), policeman, 15
la **policía** (lah po-lee-**see**-ah), policewoman, 15
el **Polo Norte** (el **po**-lo **nor**-tay), North Pole, 32
el **Polo Sur** (el **po**-lo soor), South Pole, 32

el polvo (el **pol**-bo), dust, 4; powder, 12
el pollito (el po-**yee**-to), chick, 9
el pollo (el po-yo), chicken, 10
ponerse de pie (po-**ner**-say day **pyay**), stand
   up, 27
el portero (el por-**tay**-ro), doorman, 15
la portilla (lah port-**tee**-yah), porthole, 22
el pote (el po-tay), pot, 24
el potro (el po-tro), colt, 9
el pozo (el po-so), well, 24
el precio (el **pray**-syo), price, 6
preposiciones (pray-po-see-**syo**-nes),
   prepositions, 26
la prima (lah **pree**-mah), cousin (female), 29
la primavera (lah pree-mah-**bay**-rah), spring, 5
primero (pree-**may**-ro), first, 31
el primo (el **pree**-mo), cousin (male), 29
la princesa (lah preen-**say**-sah), princess, 25
el príncipe (el **preen**-see-pay), prince, 25
los prismáticos (los prees-**mah**-tee-kos),
   binoculars, 17
la probeta (lah pro-**bay**-tah), beaker, 23
el problema aritmético (el pro-**blay**-mah
   ah-reet-**may**-tee-ko), arithmetic problem, 1
el procesador de alimentos (el pro-say-sah-**dor**
   day ah-lee-**men**-tos), food processor, 3
la programadora de computadoras (lah
   pro-grah-mah-**do**-rah day
   kom-poo-tah-**do**-rahs), computer
   programmer, 15
el prolongador (el pro-lon-gah-**dor**), protractor, 1
el proyector de película (el pro-yek-**tor** day
   pay-**lee**-koo-lah), movie projector, 4
el proyector de teatro (el pro-yek-**tor** day
   tay-**ah**-tro), spotlight, 19
el pterodáctilo (el ptay-ro-**dahk**-tee-lo),
   pterodactyl, 24
el público (el **poo**-blee-ko), audience, 19
el puente (el **pwen**-tay), bridge, 16
el puente levadizo (el **pwen**-tay
   lay-bah-**dee**-so), drawbridge, 25
la puerta (lah **pwer**-tah), door, 2; gate, 17
el pulgar (el **pool**-gar), thumb, 11
el pulpo (el **pool**-po), octopus, 22
la pulsera (lah pool-**say**-rah), bracelet, 7
la punta de flecha (lah **poon**-tah day
   flay-chah), arrowhead, 24
puntiagudo (poon-tyah-**goo**-do), sharp, 26
el pupitre (el poo-**pee**-tray), pupil desk, 1

el queso (el **kay**-so), cheese, 6
quince (**keen**-say), fifteen, 31
quinto (**keen**-to), fifth, 31

el radio (el **rrah**-dyo), radio, 2
la rama (lah **rrah**-mah), branch, 5
la rana (lah **rrah**-nah), frog, 9
la ranura (lah rrah-**noo**-rah), mail slot, 13
rápido (**rrah**-pee-do), fast, 26
la raqueta (lah rrah-**kay**-tah), racket, 18
la raqueta de tenis (lah rrah-**kay**-tah day
   tay-nees), tennis racket, 17
el rascacielos (el rras-kah-**syay**-los), skyscraper,
   8
el rastrillo (el rras-**tree**-yo), rake, 5
la rata (lah **rrah**-tah), rat, 25
el ratón (el rrah-**ton**), mouse, 9, 26
la raya (lah **rrah**-yah), part (hair), 12
las rayas (lahs **rrah**-yahs), stripes, 20
los rayos (los **rrah**-yos), spokes, 14
los rayos X (los **rrah**-yos ay-kees), X ray, 11
la recepcionista (lah rray-sep-syo-**nees**-tah),
   receptionist, 13

recibir (rray-see-**beer**), receive, 27
recoger (rray-ko-**her**), catch, 27
el rectángulo (el rrek-**tan**-goo-lo), rectangle, 30
la red (lah rred), net, 18
la red de seguridad (lah rred day
   say-goo-ree-**dahd**), safety net, 21
los reflectores (los rray-flek-**to**-res), reflectors,
   14
el refresco (el rray-**fres**-ko), soft drink, 10
la regadera (lah rray-gah-**day**-rah), sprinkler, 5
el regalo (el rray-**gah**-lo), gift, 10
regar (rray-**gar**), water, 27
el registro de equipaje (el rray-**hees**-tro day
   ay-kee-**pah**-hay), baggage check-in, 17
la regla (lah **rray**-glah), ruler, 1
la reina (lah **rray**-nah), queen, 25
reírse (rray-**eer**-say), laugh, 27
el relámpago (el rray-**lahm**-pah-go), lightning,
   5
el reloj (el rray-**loh**), clock, 1; watch, 7
el remitente (el rray-mee-**ten**-tay), return
   address, 13
el remo (el **rray**-mo), oar, 16
el reparador de televisión (el rray-pah-rah-**dor**
   day tay-lay-bee-**syon**), television repairer, 15
el restaurante (el rres-tow-**rahn**-tay),
   restaurant, 8, 10
las revistas (lahs rray-**bees**-tahs), magazines, 11
el rey (el rray), king, 25
las riendas (lahs **rryen**-dahs), reins, 25
el rimel (el **rree**-mel), mascara, 12
el rinoceronte (el rree-no-say-**ron**-tay),
   rhinoceros, 20
el río (el **rree**-o), river, 32
rizado (rree-**sah**-do), curly, 12
el rizador (el rree-sah-**dor**), curling iron, 12
el robot (el rro-**bot**), robot, 23
la roca (lah **rro**-kah), boulder, 24
la rodilla (lah rro-**dee**-yah), knee, 11
rojo (**rro**-ho), red, 28
los rollos (los **rro**-yos), curlers, 12
el rompecabezas (el rrom-pay-kah-**bay**-sahs),
   jigsaw puzzle, 4
romper (rrom-**per**), break, 27
la ropa (lah **rro**-pah), clothing, 7
la ropa interior (lah **rro**-pah een-tay-**ryor**),
   underwear, 7
la ropa sucia (lah **ro**-pah **soo**-syah), laundry, 3
el ropero (el rro-**pay**-ro), closet, 2
rosado (rro-**sah**-do), pink, 28
el rover lunar (el **rro**-ber loo-**nar**), lunar rover,
   23
rubio (**rroo**-byo), blond, 12
la rueda (lah **rrway**-dah), wheel, 24
las ruedas de entrenamiento (lahs **rrway**-das
   day ayn-tray-nah-**myen**-to), training wheels,
   14
rugir (rroo-**heer**), roar, 27

la sábana (lah **sah**-bah-nah), sheet, 2
el sacapuntas (el sah-kah-**poon**-tahs), pencil
   sharpener, 1
el saco de dormir (el **sah**-ko day dor-**meer**),
   sleeping bag, 9
la sal (lah sahl), salt, 10
la sala (lah **sah**-lah), living room, 2
la sala de espera (lah **sah**-lah day es-**pay**-rah),
   waiting room, 11
las salchichas (lahs sahl-**chee**-chahs), sausages,
   10
la salsa de tomate (lah **sahl**-sah day
   to-**mah**-tay), ketchup, 10
el saltamontes (el sal-tah-**mon**-tes),
   grasshopper, 5

saltar (sahl-**tar**), jump, 27
saltar al agua (sahl-**tar** ahl ah-gwah), dive, 27
el salto al agua (el **sahl**-to ahl ah-gwah),
   diving, 18
el salto alto (el **sahl**-to **ahl**-to), high jump, 18
el salto largo (el **sahl**-to **lar**-go), long jump, 18
el salto libre con paracaídas (el **sahl**-to
   lee-bray kon pah-rah-kah-**ee**-dahs),
   skydiving, 18
el salto mortal (el **sahl**-to mor-**tahl**),
   somersault, 21
las sandalias (lahs sahn-**dah**-lyahs), sandals, 7
la sandía (lah sahn-**dee**-ah), watermelon, 6
la sangre (lah **sahn**-gray), blood, 11
la sartén (lah sar-**ten**), pan, 3
el sastre (el **sahs**-tray), tailor, 15
el satélite (el sah-**tay**-lee-tay), satellite, 23
el saxofón (el sah-gso-**fon**), saxophone, 19
el secador (el say-kah-**dor**), blow dryer, hair
   dryer, 12
la secadora (lah say-kah-**do**-rah), clothes dryer, 3
la sección de equipaje (lah sek-**syon** day
   ay-kee-**pah**-hay), luggage compartment, 17
seco (**say**-ko), dry, 26
la secretaria (lah say-kray-**tah**-ryah), secretary,
   15
la seda dental (lah **say**-dah den-**tahl**), dental
   floss, 11
segundo (say-**goon**-do), second, 31
seis (says), six, 31
la selva (lah **sel**-bah), jungle, 32
el sello (el **say**-yo), stamp, 13
el sello de goma (el **say**-yo day **go**-mah), rubber
   stamp, 13
el semáforo (el say-**mah**-fo-ro), traffic lights, 8, 16
sentarse (sen-**tar**-say), sit down, 27
la señal (lah say-**nyahl**), sign, 8
la señal de alto (lah say-**nyahl** day **ahl**-to), stop
   sign, 16
señalar (say-nyah-**lar**), point (at), 27
séptimo (**sep**-tee-mo), seventh, 31
la serpiente (lah ser-**pyen**-tay), snake, 20
el servicio para automovilistas (el ser-**bee**-syo
   pah-rah ow-to-mo-bee-**lees**-tahs), drive-in, 13
la servilleta (lah ser-bee-**yay**-tah), napkin, 10
sesenta (say-**sen**-tah), sixty, 31
sesenta y cinco (say-**sen**-tah ee **seen**-ko),
   sixty-five, 31
sesenta y cuatro (say-**sen**-tah ee **kwah**-tro),
   sixty-four, 31
sesenta y dos (say-**sen**-tah ee **dos**), sixty-two, 31
sesenta y nueve (say-**sen**-tah ee **nway**-bay),
   sixty-nine, 31
sesenta y ocho (say-**sen**-tah ee **o**-cho),
   sixty-eight, 31
sesenta y seis (say-**sen**-tah ee **says**), sixty-six, 31
sesenta y siete (say-**sen**-tah ee **syay**-tay),
   sixty-seven, 31
sesenta y tres (say-**sen**-tah ee **tres**), sixty-three,
   31
sesenta y uno (say-**sen**-tah ee **oo**-no), sixty-one,
   31
setenta (say-**ten**-tah), seventy, 31
setenta y cinco (say-**ten**-tah ee **seen**-ko),
   seventy-five, 31
setenta y cuatro (say-**ten**-tah ee **kwah**-tro),
   seventy-four, 31
setenta y dos (say-**ten**-tah ee **dos**), seventy-two,
   31
setenta y nueve (say-**ten**-tah ee **nway**-bay),
   seventy-nine, 31
setenta y ocho (say-**ten**-tah ee **o**-cho),
   seventy-eight, 31
setenta y seis (say-**ten**-tah ee **says**), seventy-six,
   31

setenta y siete (say-**ten**-tah ee **syay**-tay), seventy-seven, 31

setenta y tres (say-**ten**-tah ee tres), seventy-three, 31

setenta y uno (say-**ten**-tah ee **oo**-no), seventy-one, 31

sexto (**ses**-to), sixth, 31

la sierra (lah **syay**-rrah), saw, 3

siete (**syay**-tay), seven, 31

la silla (lah **see**-yah), chair, 3

la silla de montar (lah **see**-yah day mon-**tar**), saddle, 25

la silla de ruedas (lah **see**-yah day **rrway**-dahs), wheelchair, 11

el sillón (el see-**yon**), armchair, 2

sin punta (seen **poon**-tah), dull, 26

el sistema solar (el sees-**tay**-mah so-**lar**), solar system, 23

sobre (**so**-bray), above, 26

el sofá (el so-**fah**), sofa, 2

el sol (el sol), sun, 23

los soldados de juego (los sol-**dah**-dos day **hway**-go), toy soldiers, 4

la sombra (lah **som**-brah), shadow, 9

el sombrero (el som-**bray**-ro), hat, 4, 7

el sombrero de copa (el som-**bray**-ro day **ko**-pah), top hat, 4

el sombrero de vaquero (el som-**bray**-ro day bah-**kay**-ro), cowboy hat, 4

la sonrisa (lah son-**rree**-sah), smile, 11

la sopa (lah **so**-pah), soup, 10

el soporte (el so-**por**-tay), kickstand, 14

la sortija (lah sor-**tee**-hah), ring, 7

suave (**swa**-bay), soft, 26

el sube y baja (el **soo**-bay ee **bah**-hah), seesaw, 8

subir (soo-**beer**), climb, 27

el submarino (el soob-mah-**ree**-no), submarine, 22

sucio (**soo**-syo), dirty, 26

sudeste (soo-**des**-tay), southeast, 32

sudoeste (soo-**does**-tay), southwest, 32

el suéter (el **sway**-ter), sweater, 7

el sujetapapeles (el soo-hay-tah-pah-**pay**-les), paper clip, 13

el supermercado (el soo-per-mer-**kah**-do), supermarket, 6

sur (soor), south, 32

el surtidor de gasolina (el soor-tee-**dor** day gah-so-**lee**-nah), gas pump, 14

la tabla (lah **tah**-blah), board, 3

la tabla de patines (lah **tah**-blah day pah-**tee**-nes), skateboard, 16

el tablero de control (el tah-**blay**-ro day kon-**trol**), control panel, 23

el tablero de instrumentos (el tah-**blay**-ro day eens-troo-**men**-tos), dashboard, 14

el tablero solar (el tah-**blay**-ro so-**lar**), solar panel, 23

el tablón de noticias (el tah-**blon** day no-**tee**-syahs), bulletin board, 1

la taladradora de papel (lah tah-lah-drah-**do**-rah day pah-**pel**), hole punch, 1

el taladro (el tah-**lah**-dro), drill, 3

el talonario de cheques (el tah-lo-**nah**-ryo day **chay**-kes), checkbook, 13

el tallo (el **tah**-yo), stem, 5

el tambor (el tahm-**bor**), drum, 19

el tampón de entintar (el tahm-**pon** day en-teen-**tar**), ink pad, 13

el tanque de oxígeno (el **tahn**-kay day o-**gsee**-hay-no), oxygen tank, 22

la tapa de registro (lah **tah**-pah day ray-**hees**-tro), manhole cover, 8

el tapacubos (el tah-pah-**koo**-bos), hubcap, 14

la taquilla (lah tah-**kee**-yah), ticket booth, 21

la tarjeta de crédito (lah tar-**hay**-tah day **kray**-dee-to), credit card, 13

la tarjeta postal (lah tar-**hay**-tah pos-**tahl**), postcard, 13

la tarta (lah **tar**-tah), cake, 10

el taxi (el **tah**-gsee), taxi, 16

el taxista (el tah-**gsees**-tah), taxi driver, 15

la taza (lah **tah**-sah), cup, 10

el tazón (el tah-**son**), bowl, 10

el té (el tay), tea, 10

el techo (el **tay**-cho), ceiling, 2

el techo de sol (el **tay**-cho day sol), sunroof, 14

el tejado (el tay-**hah**-do), roof, 2

la tejedora (lah tay-hay-**do**-rah), weaver, 24

la tela (lah **tay**-lah), cloth, 24

el telar (el tay-**lar**), loom, 24

la telaraña (lah tay-lah-**rah**-nyah), cobweb, spiderweb, 4, 25

el teléfono (el tay-**lay**-fo-no), telephone, 2

la televisión (lah tay-lay-bee-**syon**), television, 2

el telón (el tay-**lon**), curtain, 19

el témpano (el **tem**-pah-no), iceberg, 32

el tenedor (el tay-nay-**dor**), fork, 10

el tenis (el **tay**-nees), tennis, 18

el tenis de mesa (el **tay**-nees day **may**-sah), table tennis, 18

el tentáculo (el ten-**tah**-koo-lo), tentacle, 22

tercero (ter-**say**-ro), third, 31

el termómetro (el ter-**mo**-may-tro), thermometer, 11

el tesoro (el tay-**so**-ro), treasure, 22

la tetera (lah tay-**tay**-rah), kettle, 3

la tía (lah **tee**-ah), aunt, 29

el tiburón (el tee-boo-**ron**), shark, 22

el tiempo (el **tyem**-po), weather, 5

la tienda de campaña (lah **tyen**-dah day kahm-**pah**-nyah), tent, 9

la tienda de comestibles (lah **tyen**-dah day ko-mes-**tee**-bles), grocery store, 8

la tienda mayor del circo (lah **tyen**-dah mah-**yor** del **seer**-ko), big top, 21

la tierra (lah **tyay**-rrah), dirt, 9

la Tierra (lah **tyay**-rrah), Earth, 23

el tigre (el **tee**-gray), tiger, 20

el tigre de dientes de sable (el **tee**-gray day **dyen**-tes day **sah**-blay), saber-toothed tiger, 24

las tijeras (lahs tee-**hay**-rahs), scissors, 1, 12

el timón (el tee-**mon**), helm, 22

la tina (lah **tee**-nah), bathtub, 2

el tío (el **tee**-o), uncle, 29

tirar (tee-**rar**), pull, 27; throw, 27

el títere (el **tee**-tay-ray), puppet, 4

la tiza (lah **tee**-sah), chalk, 1

la toalla (lah to-**ah**-yah), towel, 2

las toallas de papel (lahs to-**ah**-yas day pah-**pel**), paper towels, 3

el tobillo (el to-**bee**-yo), ankle, 11

el tobogán (el to-bo-**gahn**), slide, 8

el tocadiscos (el to-kah-**dees**-kos), record player, 2

el tocador (el to-kah-**dor**), dresser, 2

tocar (to-**kar**), play (an instrument), 27

los tomates (los to-**mah**-tes), tomatoes, 6

la tormenta de nieve (lah tor-**men**-tah day **nyay**-bay), snowstorm, 5

el tornillo (el tor-**nee**-yo), screw, 3

el torno de hilar (el **tor**-no day ee-**lar**), spinning wheel, 4

el toro (el **to**-ro), bull, 9

la toronja (lah to-**ron**-hah), grapefruit, 6

la torre (lah **to**-rray), tower, 25

la torre de control (lah **to**-rray day kon-**trol**), control tower, 17

la tortilla (lah tor-**tee**-yah), omelet, 10

la tortuga (lah tor-**too**-gah), turtle, 20

la tortuga de mar (lah tor-**too**-gah day mar), sea turtle, 22

la tostada (lah tos-**tah**-dah), toast, 10

el tostador (el tos-tah-**dor**), toaster, 3

la trabajadora de fábrica (lah trah-bah-hah-**do**-rah day **fah**-bree-kah), factory worker, 15

el tractor (el trak-**tor**), tractor, 9

el traje (el **trah**-hay), suit, 7

el traje de baño (el **trah**-hay day **bah**-nyo), bathing suit, 7

el traje de goma (el **trah**-hay day **go**-mah), wet suit, 22

el traje de malla (el **trah**-hay day **mah**-yah), tights, 7

el traje espacial (el **trah**-hay es-pah-**syahl**), space suit, 23

el transporte (el trans-**por**-tay), transportation, 16

el trapeador (el trah-pay-ah-**dor**), mop, 3

el trapecio (el trah-**pay**-syo), trapeze, 21

el trapecista (el trah-pay-**sees**-tah), trapeze artist, 21

el trapo (el **trah**-po), rag, 14

trece (**tray**-say), thirteen, 31

treinta (**trayn**-tah), thirty, 31

treinta y cinco (**trayn**-tah ee **seen**-ko), thirty-five, 31

treinta y cuatro (**trayn**-tah ee **kwah**-tro), thirty-four, 31

treinta y dos (**trayn**-tah ee dos), thirty-two, 31

treinta y nueve (**trayn**-tah ee **nway**-bay), thirty-nine, 31

treinta y ocho (**trayn**-tah ee **o**-cho), thirty-eight, 31

treinta y seis (**trayn**-tah ee says), thirty-six, 31

treinta y siete (**trayn**-tah ee **syay**-tay), thirty-seven, 31

treinta y tres (**trayn**-tah ee tres), thirty-three, 31

treinta y uno (**trayn**-tah ee **oo**-no), thirty-one, 31

el tren (el tren), train, 16

el tren de aterrizaje (el tren day ah-tay-rree-**sah**-hay), landing gear, 17

el tren eléctrico (el tren ay-**lek**-tree-ko), electric train, 4

la trenza (lah **tren**-sah), braid, 12

tres (tres), three, 31

el triángulo (el tree-**ahn**-goo-lo), triangle, 30

el triciclo (el tree-**see**-klo), tricycle, 14

el trigo (el **tree**-go), wheat, 24

el trineo (el tree-**nay**-o), sled, 5

triste (**trees**-tay), sad, 26

el trofeo (el tro-**fay**-o), trophy, 18

el trombón (el trom-**bon**), trombone, 19

la trompa (lah **trom**-pah), trunk (mammoth), 24

la trompeta (lah trom-**pay**-tah), trumpet, 19

el tronco (el **tron**-ko), log, 5

el trono (el **tro**-no), throne, 25

el trovador (el tro-bah-**dor**), minstrel, 25

la tuba (lah **too**-bah), tuba, 19

el tubo de ensayo (el **too**-bo day en-**sah**-yo), test tube, 23

la tundra (lah **toon**-drah), tundra, 32

el turbante (el toor-**bahn**-tay), turban, 21

el tutú (el too-**too**), tutu, 19

el unicornio (el oo-nee-**kor**-nyo), unicorn, 25

el uniforme (el oo-nee-**for**-may), uniform, 4

uno (**oo**-no), one, 31
la **uña** (lah **oo**-nyah), fingernail, 12; (**del pie**), toenail, 12
las **uvas** (las **oo**-bahs), grapes, 6

la **vaca** (lah **bah**-kah), cow, 9
vacío (bah-**see**-o), empty, 26
las **vallas** (lahs **bah**-yas), hurdles, 18
el **vaquero** (el bah-**kay**-ro), cowboy, 15
los **vaqueros** (los bah-**kay**-ros), jeans, 7
la **vara** (lah **bah**-rah), baton, 21
la **varilla mágica** (lah bah-**ree**-yah **mah**-hee-kah), magic wand, 25
el **vaso** (el **bah**-so), glass, 10
veinte (**bayn**-tay), twenty, 31
veinticinco (bayn-tee-**seen**-ko), twenty-five, 31
veinticuatro (bayn-tee-**kwah**-tro), twenty-four, 31
veintidós (bayn-tee-**dos**), twenty-two, 31
veintinueve (bayn-tee-**nway**-bay), twenty-nine, 31
veintiocho (bayn-tee-**o**-cho), twenty-eight, 31
veintiséis (bayn-tee-**says**), twenty-six, 31
veintisiete (bayn-tee-**syay**-tay), twenty-seven, 31
veintitrés (bayn-tee-**tres**), twenty-three, 31

veintiuno (bayn-tee-**oo**-no), twenty-one, 31
la **vela** (lah **bay**-lah), candle, 10; sail, 16
la **venda adhesiva** (lah **ben**-dah ah-day-**see**-bah), bandage, 11
el **vendedor** (el ben-day-**dor**), salesman, 15
el **vendedor de boletos** (el ben-day-**dor** day bo-**lay**-tos), ticket agent, 17
la **vendedora** (lah ben-day-**do**-rah), saleswoman, 15
vender (ben-**der**), sell, 27
venir (bay-**neer**), come, 27
la **ventana** (lah ben-**tah**-nah), window, 2
el **ventilador** (el ben-tee-lah-**dor**), fan, 5
el **verano** (el bay-**rah**-no), summer, 5
verde (**ber**-day), green, 28
el **vestido** (el bes-**tee**-do), dress, 7
el **vestido de baile** (el bes-**tee**-do day **bigh**-lay), ball gown, 4
la **veterinaria** (lah bay-tay-ree-**nah**-ryah), veterinarian, 15
las **vías de ferrocarril** (lahs **bee**-ahs day fay-rro-kah-**rreel**), train tracks, 9
viejo (**byay**-ho), old, 26
el **viento** (el **byen**-to), wind, 5
la **villa** (lah **bee**-yah), village, 24
el **violín** (el byo-**leen**), violin, 19

el **violoncelo** (el byo-lon-**say**-lo), cello, 19
el **volante** (el bo-**lahn**-tay), steering wheel, 14
volar (bo-**lar**), fly, 27
el **volcán** (el bol-**kahn**), volcano, 32
el **voleibol** (el **bo**-lay-bol), volleyball, 18
la **voltereta lateral** (lah bol-tay-**ray**-tah lah-tay-**rahl**), cartwheel, 21
el **vuelo espacial** (el **bway**-lo es-pah-**syahl**), space shuttle, 23

el **xilófono** (el see-**lo**-fo-no), xylophone, 19

la **yema** (lah **yay**-mah), yolk, 10
el **yunque** (el **yoon**-kay), anvil, 25

las **zanahorias** (lahs sah-nah-**o**-ryahs), carrots, 6
los **zancos** (los **sahn**-kos), stilts, 21
las **zapatillas de ballet** (lahs sah-pah-**tee**-yahs day bah-**let**), ballet slippers, 19
los **zapatos** (los sah-**pah**-tos), shoes, 7
los **zapatos de tenis** (los sah-**pah**-tos day **tay**-nees), gym shoes, 7
el **zorro** (el **so**-rro), fox, 20

English-Spanish Glossary and Index

above, sobre, 26
accordion, el acordeón, 19
acrobat, el acróbata, 21
action, la acción, 27
actor, el actor, 19
actress, la actriz, 19
address, la dirección, 13
adjectives, adjetivos, 26
Africa, África, 32
air hose, la manga de aire, 14
airplane, el avión, 16, 17
airport, el aeropuerto, 17
air-traffic controller, la controladora de tráfico, 17
alarm clock, el despertador, 2
alien, el extraterrestre, 23
alligator, el caimán, 20
alphabet, el alfabeto, 1
ambulance, la ambulancia, 16
anchor, el ancla, 22
angelfish, el angelote, 22
animals, los animales, 20
ankle, el tobillo, 11
ant, la hormiga, 9
Antarctica, la Antártida, 32
antenna, la antena, 23
anvil, el yunque, 25
apartment building, el edificio de apartamentos, 8
apple, la manzana, 6
apron, el delantal, 3
aquarium, el acuario, 1
archer, el arquero, 25
architect, la arquitecta, 15
Arctic Ocean, el Océano Glacial Ártico, 32
arithmetic problem, el problema aritmético, 1
arm, el brazo, 11
armchair, el sillón, 2
armor, la armadura, 25
arrow, la flecha, 25
arrowhead, la punta de flecha, 24
artist, la artista, 15
Asia, Asia, 32
asteroid, el asteroide, 23
astronaut, el astronauta, 23
astronomer, el astrónomo, 15
athlete, el atleta, 15
Atlantic Ocean, el Océano Atlántico, 32
attic, el desván, 4
audience, el público, 19
auditorium, el auditorio, 19
aunt, la tía, 29
Australia, Australia, 32
automatic teller, el cajero automático, 13
avocado, el aguacate, 6
ax, el hacha, 25

baby, el bebé, 9
baby carriage, el cochecito, 16
back, la espalda, 11
backpack, la mochila, 7
backseat, el asiento posterior, 14
bad, malo, 26
badminton, el badminton, 18
baggage cart, el carrito de equipaje, 17
baggage check-in, el registro de equipaje, 17
baggage claim, la contraseña de equipaje, 17
baggage handler, el mozo de equipaje, 17
bakery, la pastelería, 8
balcony, el balcón, 8
bald, calvo, 12
ball gown, el vestido de baile, 4
ballet slippers, las zapatillas de ballet, 19
balloon, el globo, 21
banana, el plátano, 6
band, la banda, 21
bandage, la venda adhesiva, 11
bangs, el flequillo, 12
bank, el banco, 13
banker, la banquera, 15
banner, el estandarte, 25

barbecue, la barbacoa, 5
barber, el barbero, 12
barber shop, la peluquería de caballeros, 12
bareback rider, la jinete, 21
barn, el granero, 9
barnacle, el percebe, 22
barrette, el pasador, 12
baseball (game), el béisbol, 18; (ball), la pelota (de béisbol), 18
basket, la canasta, 24
basketball, el baloncesto, 18
bat (baseball), el bate, 18; (animal), el murciélago, 25
bathing suit, el traje de baño, 7
bathrobe, la bata, 7
bathroom, el cuarto de baño, 2
bathtub, la tina, 2
baton, la vara, 21
bay, la bahía, 32
beach, la playa, 8
beak, el pico, 20
beaker, la probeta, 23
bear, el oso, 20
bear cub, el cachorro de oso, 20
beard, la barba, 12
beauty salon, la peluquería de señoras, 12
bed, la cama, 2
bedroom, el dormitorio, 2
bees, las abejas, 9
behind, detrás de, 26
bell, la campana, 1
belt, el cinturón, 7
bench, el banco, 8
between, entre, 26
bicycle, la bicicleta, 14, 16, 18
bicycle chain, la cadena de bicicleta, 14
big top, la tienda mayor del circo, 21
bill, el billete, 13
billion, mil millones, 31
binoculars, los prismáticos, 17
bird, el pájaró, 5
bird's nest, el nido de pájaro, 5
birthday party, la fiesta de cumpleaños, 10
bison, el bisonte, 24
black, negro, 12, 28
blacksmith, el herrero, 25
blanket, la manta, 2
blimp, el dirigible, 16
blocks, los cubos, 4
blond, rubio, 12
blood, la sangre, 11
blouse, la blusa, 7
blow dryer, el secador, 12
blue, azul, 28
board, la tabla, 3
boat, el barco, 16
bone, el hueso, 24
book, el libro, 1
bookcase, la estantería, 1
bookseller, el librero, 15
bookstore, la librería, 8
boots, las botas, 7
bottle, la botella, 6
bottom, de abajo, 26
boulder, la roca, 24
bow (knot), el lazo, 13; (violin), el arco, 19; (weapon), el arco, 25
bowl, el tazón, 10
bowling, jugar a los bolos, 18
box, la caja, 4
boxing, el boxeo, 18
boxing gloves, los guantes de boxeo, 18
boy, el niño, 9
bracelet, la pulsera, 7
braces, los frenos, 11
braid, la trenza, 12
brake lights, los faros de freno, 14
branch, la rama, 5
bread, el pan, 6
break, romper, 27

breakfast, el desayuno, 10
brick, el ladrillo, 3
bridge, el puente, 16
briefcase, la cartera, 17
broccoli, el bróculi, 10
broom, la escoba, 3
brother, el hermano, 29
brown, moreno, 12; café, 28
brush, el cepillo, 12
bubble, la burbuja, 22
bucket, el balde, 24
buckle, la hebilla, 7
building, el edificio, 8
bull, el toro, 9
bulletin board, el tablón de noticias, 1
bun (hair), el moño, 12
buoy, la boya, 22
bus, el autobús, 16
bus driver, la conductora de autobús, 15
bus stop, la parada de autobús, 16
bush, el arbusto, 5
butcher, el carnicero, 15
butcher shop, la carnicería, 8
butter, la mantequilla, 6
butterfly, la mariposa, 5
button, el botón, 7
buy, comprar, 27
cabbage, la col, 6
cactus, el cacto, 1
cage, la jaula, 21
cake, la tarta, 10
calculator, la calculadora, 1
calendar, el calendario, 1
calf, el becerro, 9
camel, el camello, 20
camera, la cámara, 17, 21
camper, la caravana, 16
can, la lata, 6
canal, el canal, 32
candle, la vela, 10
candy, los dulces, 6
cane, el bastón, 11
cannon, el cañón, 22
canoe, la canoa, 16
cap, el gorro, 7
cape (clothing), la capa, 21; (geography), el cabo, 32
car, el coche, 16
car racing, las carreras de coches, 18
car wash, el lavado de coches, 14
caramel apple, la manzana de caramelo, 21
cardinal numbers, los números cardinales, 31
cards, los naipes, 4
cargo bay, el compartimiento de flete, 23
carpenter, el carpintero, 15
carpet, la alfombra, 2
carrots, las zanahorias, 6
carry, llevar, 27
cart, la carreta, 24
cartwheel, la voltereta lateral, 21
cash register, la caja, 6
cashier, la cajera, 6
cassette player, la grabadora, 2
cassette tape, el casete, 2
cast, la escayola, 11
castle, el castillo, 25
cat, el gato, 9
catch, recoger, 27
cave, la caverna, 24
cave drawing, el dibujo de caverna, 24
cave dwellers, los cavernícolas, 24
ceiling, el techo, 2
celery, el apio, 6
cello, el violoncelo, 19
cellophane tape, la cinta adhesiva, 1
cement mixer, el mezclador de cemento, 16
cereal, el cereal, 6
chain mail, la cota de mallas, 25
chair, la silla, 3
chalk, la tiza, 1

chalkboard, la pizarra, 1
channel, el canal, 32
check, el cheque, 13
checkbook, el talonario de cheques, 13
checkers, el juego de damas, 4
cheek, la mejilla, 11
cheese, el queso, 6
cherries, las cerezas, 6
chess, el ajedrez, 4
chest, el pecho, 11
chick, el pollito, 9
chicken, el pollo, 10
children, los niños, 19
chimney, la chimenea, 2
chin, la barbilla, 11
chocolate, el chocolate, 6
church, la iglesia, 8
circle, el círculo, 30
circus, el circo, 21
circus parade, el desfile del circo, 21
city, la ciudad, 8
clam, la almeja, 22
clarinet, el clarinete, 19
classroom, el aula, 1
claws, las garras, 20
clay, el barro, 24
clean, limpio, 26
climb, subir, 27
clock, el reloj, 1
close, cerrar, 27
closed, cerrado, 26
closet, el ropero, 2
cloth, la tela, 24
clothes dryer, la secadora, 3
clothing, la ropa, 7
clothing store, el almacén, 8
clouds, las nubes, 5
clown, la payasa, 21
club, el palo, 24
coat, el abrigo, 7
cobweb, la telaraña, 4
coffee, el café, 10
coin, la moneda, 13
cold, frío, 26
collar, el cuello, 7
colored pencils, los lápices de color, 1
coloring book, el libro de colorear, 4
colors, los colores, 28
colt, el potro, 9
comb, el peine, 12
come, venir, 27
comet, el cometa, 23
comic books, los libros de cómicos, 4
community, la comunidad, 15
compact disc, el disco compacto, 2
compass (drawing), el compás, 1; (magnetic), la
  brújula, 32
computer, la computadora, 23
computer programmer, la programadora de
  computadoras, 15
Concorde, el Concorde, 17
conductor, el director, 19
cone, el cono, 30
constellation, la constelación, 23
control panel, el tablero de control, 23
control tower, la torre de control, 17
cook, el cocinero, 15
cook (verb), cocinar, 27
cookies, las galletas dulces, 6
copilot, la copiloto, 17
coral, el coral, 22
coral reef, el arrecife de coral, 22
corn, el maíz, 24
corner, la esquina, 8
costume, el disfraz, 19
cotton candy, el algodón de azúcar, 21
counter, el mostrador, 3
country, el campo, 9
court jester, el bufón, 25
courtyard, el patio, 25
cousin (female), la prima, 29; (male), el primo, 29
coveralls, el mono, 14
cow, la vaca, 9

cowboy, el vaquero, 15
cowboy boots, las botas de vaquero, 4
cowboy hat, el sombrero de vaquero, 4
crab, el cangrejo, 22
crackers, las galletas, 6
cradle, la cuna, 4
crane, la grúa, 8
crater, el cráter, 23
crayon, el creyón, 1
cream, la crema, 10
credit card, la tarjeta de crédito, 13
crew cut, el corte a cepillo, 12
crop (farming), la cosecha, 24
cross-country skiing, el esquí nórdico, 18
crosswalk, el cruce de peatones, 16
crown, la corona, 25
cruise ship, el crucero, 16
crutch, la muleta, 11
cry, llorar, 27
cube, el cubo, 30
cup, la taza, 10
curlers, los rollos, 12
curling iron, el rizador, 12
curly, rizado, 12
curtain (in a theater), el telón, 19
curtains (in the house), las cortinas, 2
customs officer, la aduanera, 17
cut, cortar, 27
cycling, el ciclismo, 18
cylinder, el cilindro, 30
cymbals, los címbalos, 19

dad, el papá, 29
dance, bailar, 27
dancer, la bailarina, 19
dark, oscuro, 26
dashboard, el tablero de instrumentos, 14
daughter, la hija, 29
deck, el patio, 5
deer, el ciervo, 20
dental floss, la seda dental, 11
dental hygienist, la higienista dental, 11
dentist, el dentista, 11
dentist's office, la oficina del dentista, 11
desert, el desierto, 32
desk (pupil's), el pupitre, 1; (teacher's), el
  escritorio, 1
dice, los dados, 4
difficult, difícil, 26
dig, cavar, 27
dining room, el comedor, 2
dinner, la cena, 10
dinosaur, el dinosaurio, 24
dirt, la tierra, 9
dirty, sucio, 26
disc jockey, el disc jockey, 15
dishes, los platos, 3
dishwasher, el lavaplatos, 3
dive, saltar (al agua), 27
diving, el salto al agua, 18
dock, el muelle, 16
doctor, la médica, 11
doctor's office, la oficina del médico, 11
dog, el perro, 9
doll, la muñeca, 4
dollhouse, la casa de muñecas, 4
dolphin, el delfín, 22
donkey, el burro, 9
door, la puerta, 2
door handle, la manilla, 14
doorman, el portero, 15
down, abajo, 26
down vest, el chaleco de plumón, 7
downhill skiing, el esquí alpino, 18
dragon, el dragón, 25
draw, dibujar, 27
drawbridge, el puente levadizo, 25
drawer, el cajón, 3
dress, el vestido, 7
dresser, el tocador, 2
dressing room, el camarín, 19
drill, el taladro, 3
drink, beber, 27

drive, manejar, 27
drive-in, el servicio para automovilistas, 13
driver's seat, el asiento del conductor, 14
driveway, el camino particular, 8
drugstore, la farmacia, 8
drum, el tambor, 19
dry, seco, 26
duck, el pato, 9
duckling, el patito, 9
dull, sin punta, 26
dungeon, el calabozo, 25
dust, el polvo, 4
dustpan, la pala de basura, 3

eagle, el águila, 20
ear, la oreja, 11
earmuffs, las orejeras, 7
earring, el arete, 7
Earth, la Tierra, 23
easel, el caballete de pintor, 1
east, este, 32
easy, fácil, 26
eat, comer, 27
eggs, los huevos, 6
eight, ocho, 31
eighteen, dieciocho, 31
eighth, octavo, 31
eighty, ochenta, 31
eighty-eight, ochenta y ocho, 31
eighty-five, ochenta y cinco, 31
eighty-four, ochenta y cuatro, 31
eighty-nine, ochenta y nueve, 31
eighty-one, ochenta y uno, 31
eighty-seven, ochenta y siete, 31
eighty-six, ochenta y seis, 31
eighty-three, ochenta y tres, 31
eighty-two, ochenta y dos, 31
elbow, el codo, 11
electric mixer, la batidora eléctrica, 3
electric train, el tren eléctrico, 4
electrical outlet, el enchufe, 3
electrician, el electricista, 15
elephant, el elefante, 20, 21
elevator, el ascensor, 17
eleven, once, 31
elf, el duende, 25
empty, vacío, 26
engine, el motor, 14, 17
equator, el ecuador, 32
eraser (chalkboard), el borrador, 1; (pencil), la
  goma de borrar, 1
escalator, la escalera mecánica, 17
Europe, Europa, 32
examining table, la camilla, 11
eyebrow, la ceja, 11
eyes, los ojos, 11

face, la cara, 11
factory, la fábrica, 8
factory worker, la trabajadora de fábrica, 15
fairy, el hada, 25
fall (season), el otoño, 5; (verb), caerse, 27
family tree, el árbol genealógico, 29
fan (hand), el abanico, 4; (electric), el ventilador, 5
far, lejos de, 26
farm, la granja, 9
farmer, el granjero, 9
fashion designer, la diseñadora de modas, 15
fast, rápido, 26
fat, gordo, 26
father, el padre, 29
faucet, el grifo, 3
fault, la falla, 32
feather, la pluma, 4
feathers, las plumas, 20
fence, la cerca, 9
fender, el guardalodo, 14
fern, el helecho, 24
field, el campo, 24
fifteen, quince, 31
fifth, quinto, 31
fifty, cincuenta, 31

fifty-eight, cincuenta y ocho, 31
fifty-five, cincuenta y cinco, 31
fifty-four, cincuenta y cuatro, 31
fifty-nine, cincuenta y nueve, 31
fifty-one, cincuenta y uno, 31
fifty-seven, cincuenta y siete, 31
fifty-six, cincuenta y seis, 31
fifty-three, cincuenta y tres, 31
fifty-two, cincuenta y dos, 31
file, la lima, 3
file cabinet, el archivo, 13
film, la película, 21
fin, la aleta, 22
find, encontrar, 27
finger, el dedo, 11
fingernail, la uña, 12
fire, el fuego, 24
fire engine, el coche de bomberos, 16
fire escape, la escalera de incendios, 8
fire fighter, el bombero, 15
fire hydrant, la boca de incendios, 8
fire station, la estación de bomberos, 8
fireplace, la chimenea, 2
first, primero, 31
fish (in the water), el pez, 1; (cooked), el pescado, 10
fisherman, el pescador, 15
fishhook, el anzuelo, 22
fishing, la pesca, 24
fishing line, el hilo de pescar, 22
five, cinco, 31
fix, arreglar, 27
flags, las banderas, 17
flamingo, el flamenco, 20
flashbulb, la lámpara flash, 21
flashlight, la linterna eléctrica, 3
flat tire, la llanta reventada, 14
flight attendant, el auxiliar de vuelo, 17
flint, el pedernal, 24
flipper, la aleta, 22
floor, el piso, 2
florist, la florera, 15
flour, la harina, 3
flowerbed, el cuadro de jardín, 5
flowers, las flores, 5
flute, la flauta, 19
fly (insect), la mosca, 5; (verb), volar, 27
fly swatter, el matamoscas, 5
fog, la niebla, 5
food, la comida, 6
food processor, el procesador de alimentos, 3
foot, el pie, 11
football (ball), la pelota (de fútbol americano), 18; (game), el fútbol americano, 18
footprint, la huella del pie, 23
footstool, el banquillo, 2
forehead, la frente, 11
foreman, el capataz, 15
forest, el bosque, 25
forge, la fragua, 25
fork, el tenedor, 10
forty, cuarenta, 31
forty-eight, cuarenta y ocho, 31
forty-five, cuarenta y cinco, 31
forty-four, cuarenta y cuatro, 31
forty-nine, cuarenta y nueve, 31
forty-one, cuarenta y uno, 31
forty-seven, cuarenta y siete, 31
forty-six, cuarenta y seis, 31
forty-three, cuarenta y tres, 31
forty-two, cuarenta y dos, 31
fountain, la fuente, 8
four, cuatro, 31
fourteen, catorce, 31
fourth, cuarto, 31
fox, el zorro, 20
freckles, las pecas, 12
freezer, el congelador, 3
french fries, las papas fritas, 10
French horn, el corno francés, 19
frog, la rana, 9
frozen dinner, la cena congelada, 6
fruit, la fruta, 6
fruit juice, el jugo, 6

full, lleno, 26
fur, la piel, 24

galaxy, la galaxia, 23
game, el juego, 4
garage, el garaje, 14
garden hose, la manguera de jardín, 5
gardener, el jardinero, 15
garment bag, la maleta para vestidos y trajes, 17
gas cap, el casco del tanque de gasolina, 14
gas pump, el surtidor de gasolina, 14
gas station, la gasolinera, 14
gate, la puerta, 17
giant, el gigante, 25
gift, el regalo, 10
gills, las agallas, 22
giraffe, la jirafa, 20
girl, la niña, 9
give, dar, 27
glacier, el glaciar, 32
glass, el vaso, 10
glasses, los anteojos, 7
globe, el globo terráqueo, 1
gloves, los guantes, 7
glue, la cola, 1
go, ir, 27
Go!, ¡Adelante!, 16
goat, la cabra, 9
goggles, las gafas protectoras, 18
gold (metal), el oro, 22; (color) dorado, 28
golf, el golf, 18
golf club, el palo de golf, 18
good, bueno, 26
goose, el ganso, 9
gorilla, el gorila, 20
gosling, el gansarón, 9
grandfather, el abuelo, 29
grandma, la abuelita, 29
grandmother, la abuela, 29
grandpa, el abuelito, 29
grapefruit, la toronja, 6
grapes, las uvas, 6
grass, la hierba, 9
grasshopper, el saltamontes, 5
gray, gris, 28
green, verde, 28
green beans, las judías verdes, 6
grocery store, la tienda de comestibles, 8
guitar, la guitarra, 19
gulf, el golfo, 32
gym shoes, los zapatos de tenis, 7
gymnastics, la gimnasia, 18

hair, el pelo, 12
hair dryer, el secador, 12
hair spray, la laca, 12
hairstylist, la peluquera, 12
half, la mitad, 31
ham, el jamón, 10
hamburger, la hamburguesa, 10
hammer, el martillo, 3
hammock, la hamaca, 5
hand (clock), la manecilla, 1; (person) la mano, 11
hand brake, el freno manual, 14
handkerchief, el pañuelo, 7
handlebars, el manillar, 14
handstand, el farol, 21
hang glider, el planeador, 16
hangar, el hangar, 17
hanger, el colgadero, 2
happy, feliz, 26
hard, duro, 26
harp, el arpa, 19
hat, el sombrero, 4, 7
hay, la paja, 9
head, la cabeza, 11
headlight, el faro, 14
headset, el juego de auriculares, 17
headstand, la parada de cabeza, 21
heavy, pesado, 26
helicopter, el helicóptero, 16
helm, el timón, 22

helmet, el casco, 18
hen, la gallina, 9
high jump, el salto alto, 18
hiking boots, las botas de campo, 7
hill, la colina, 9
hippopotamus, el hipopótamo, 20
history, la historia, 24
hockey, el hockey, 18
hole punch, la taladradora de papel, 1
hood (clothing), la capucha, 7; (car), el capó, 14
hoof, el casco, 20
hoop, el aro, 21
horns, los cuernos, 9, 20
horse, el caballo, 9
horse racing, las carreras de caballos, 18
horseback riding, la equitación, 18
horseshoe, la herradura, 25
hospital, el hospital, 8
hot, caliente, 26
hot-air balloon, el globo, 16
hotel, el hotel, 8
house, la casa, 2
hubcap, el tapacubos, 14
human history, la historia de la humanidad, 24
hump, la giba, 20
hundred, cien, 31
hundred thousand, cien mil, 31
hunter, el cazador, 24
hurdles, las vallas, 18
hut, la cabaña, 24
hypodermic needle, la aguja hipodérmica, 11

ice, el hielo, 5
ice cream, el helado, 10
ice cubes, los cubos de hielo, 3
iceberg, el témpano, 32
icecap, el manto de hielo, 32
icicle, el carámbano, 5
in front of, enfrente de, 26
Indian Ocean, el Océano Índico, 32
ink pad, el tampón de entintar, 13
insect, el insecto, 24
inside, dentro de, 26
intersection, la intersección, 16
iron, la plancha, 3
ironing board, la mesa de planchar, 3
island, la isla, 32

jack, el gato, 14
jacket, la chaqueta, 7
jaguar, el jaguar, 20
jail, la cárcel, 8
jam, la mermelada, 10
jeans, los vaqueros, 7
jeep, el jeep, 16
jellyfish, la medusa, 22
jewel, la joya, 22
jeweler, el joyero, 15
jigsaw puzzle, el rompecabezas, 4
jogging, el jogging, 18
judge, la juez, 15
juggle, hacer juegos malabares, 27
juggler, el malabarista, 21
jump, saltar, 27
jump rope, la cuerda de brincar, 4
jungle, la selva, 32
jungle gym, las barras, 8

kangaroo, el canguro, 20
ketchup, la salsa de tomate, 10
kettle, la tetera, 3
key, la llave, 13
kick, patear, 27
kickstand, el soporte, 14
kid, el chivato, 9
kiln, el horno, 24
king, el rey, 25
kitchen, la cocina, 2, 3
kite, la cometa, 5
kitten, el gatito, 9
knee, la rodilla, 11

knife, el cuchillo, 10
knight, el caballero, 25
knitting needles, las agujas de tejer, 4
knot, el nudo, 13

lab coat, la bata de laboratorio, 23
label, la etiqueta, 13
laboratory, el laboratorio, 23
ladder, la escalera, 23
lake, el lago, 32
lamb, el cordero, 9
lamp, la lámpara, 2
lance, la lanza, 25
landing capsule, la cápsula de aterrizaje, 23
landing gear, el tren de aterrizaje, 17
large, grande, 26
laugh, reírse, 27
laundry, la ropa sucia, 3
laundry detergent, el detergente, 3
lawn mower, la cortadora de grama, 5
lawyer, la abogada, 15
leaf, la hoja, 5
leather, el cuero, 24
left, izquierdo, 26
leg, la pierna, 11
lemon, el limón, 6
leopard, el leopardo, 20
leotard, la malla, 19
letter, la carta, 13
letter carrier, el cartero, 15
lettuce, la lechuga, 6
librarian, el bibliotecario, 15
light (not dark), claro, 26; (not heavy), ligero, 26
lightbulb, la bombilla, 4, 21
lighthouse, el faro, 16
lightning, el relámpago, 5
lime, el limón verde, 6
lion, el león, 20, 21
lion tamer, el domador de fieras, 21
lips, los labios, 11
lipstick, el lápiz de labios, 12
listen (to), escuchar, 27
living room, la sala, 2
lizard, el lagarto, 20
lobster, la langosta, 22
lock, la cerradura, 13
log, el tronco, 5
long, largo, 12, 26
long jump, el salto largo, 18
look for, buscar, 27
loom, el telar, 24
loudspeaker, el altavoz, 1
luggage compartment, la sección de equipaje, 17
lunar rover, el rover lunar, 23
lunch, el almuerzo, 10

magazines, las revistas, 11
magic wand, la varilla mágica, 25
magician, el mago, 21
magnet, el imán, 4
mail slot, la ranura, 13
mailbag, la bolsa de correo, 13
mailbox, el buzón, 13
make-believe, de ficción, 25
makeup, el maquillaje, 19
mammoth, el mamut, 24
man, el hombre, 9
mane, la melena, 20
manhole cover, la tapa de registro, 8
manicurist, la manicura, 12
map, el mapa, 1
map of the world, un mapamundi, 32
marbles, las canicas, 4
mascara, el rimel, 12
mask, la máscara, 19, 22
master of ceremonies, el animador, 19
matches, los fósforos, 5
meals, las comidas, 10
meat, la carne, 6
mechanic, el mecánico, 14
medal, la medalla, 18
medicine, la medicina, 11

medicine cabinet, el gabinete de medicina, 2
medium, mediano, 26
melon, el melón, 6
menu, el menú, 10
metal detector, el indicador de metales, 17
meteor shower, la lluvia meteórica, 23
microphone, el micrófono, 19
microscope, el microscopio, 23
microwave oven, el horno de microondas, 3
milk, la leche, 6
million, un millón, 31
minstrel, el trovador, 25
mirror, el espejo, 2
mittens, las manoplas, 7
moat, el foso, 25
model, la modelo, 15
mom, la mamá, 29
money, el dinero, 6
monkey, el mono, 20
moon, la luna, 23
moon rock, la piedra de luna, 23
mop, el trapeador, 3
mother, la madre, 29
motorboat, la lancha, 16
motorcycle, la motocicleta, 16
mountains, las montañas, 32
mouse, el ratón, 9, 26
mousse, la espuma de pelo, 12
mouth, la boca, 11
movie projector, el proyector de película, 4
movie theater, el cine, 8
mud, el lodo, 5
museum, el museo, 8
mushroom, el hongo, 10
music box, la cajita de música, 4
mustache, el bigote, 12
mustard, la mostaza, 10

nail, el clavo, 3
nail clippers, el cortaúñas, 12
nail file, la lima, 12
nail polish, el esmalte, 12
napkin, la servilleta, 10
narrow, estrecho, 26
navigator, el navegante, 17
near, cerca de, 26
nebula, la nebulosa, 23
necklace, el collar, 7
nest, el nido, 5
net, la red, 18
new, nuevo, 26
newspaper, el periódico, 8
next to, al lado de, 26
night, la noche, 21
night table, la mesa de noche, 2
nine, nueve, 31
nineteen, diecinueve, 31
ninety, noventa, 31
ninety-eight, noventa y ocho, 31
ninety-five, noventa y cinco, 31
ninety-four, noventa y cuatro, 31
ninety-nine, noventa y nueve, 31
ninety-one, noventa y uno, 31
ninety-seven, noventa y siete, 31
ninety-six, noventa y seis, 31
ninety-three, noventa y tres, 31
ninety-two, noventa y dos, 31
ninth, noveno, 31
noodles, los fideos, 10
north, norte, 32
North America, la América del Norte, 32
North Pole, el Polo Norte, 32
northeast, nordeste, 32
northwest, noroeste, 32
nose, la nariz, 11
notebook, el cuaderno, 1
notepad, el cuaderno, 13
numbers, los números, 1, 31
nurse, el enfermero, 11
nuts, las nueces, 6

oar, el remo, 16

oasis, el oasis, 32
ocean, el mar, 22
octagon, el octágono, 30
octopus, el pulpo, 22
off, apagado, 26
oil, el aceite, 14
old, viejo, 26
omelet, la tortilla, 10
on, encendido, 26
on top of, encima de, 26
one, uno, 31
onions, las cebollas, 6
open (verb), abrir, 27; (adjective), abierto, 26
optician, la oculista, 15
orange (fruit), la naranja, 6; (color), anaranjado, 28
orchestra, la orquesta, 19
orchestra pit, el foso de la orquesta, 19
ordinal numbers, los números ordinales, 31
ostrich, el avestruz, 20
outside, fuera de, 26
oval, el óvalo, 30
oven, el horno, 3
owl, la lechuza, 20
oxygen tank, el tanque de oxígeno, 22

Pacific Ocean, el Océano Pacífico, 32
package, el paquete, 13
packing tape, la cinta, 13
paint, la pintura, 1, 24
paint, pintar, 27
paintbrush, el pincel, 1
painter, el pintor, 15
pajamas, el pijama, 7
pan, la sartén, 3
panda, el panda, 20
pants, los pantalones, 7
paper, el papel, 1
paper clip, el sujetapapeles, 13
paper towels, las toallas de papel, 3
parachute, el paracaídas, 18
paramedic, el auxiliar del médico, 15
park, el parque, 8
parking lot, el aparcamiento, 8
parking meter, el parquímetro, 8
parrot, el loro, 20
part (hair), la raya, 12
passenger, el pasajero, 17
passenger's seat, el asiento del pasajero, 14
passport, el pasaporte, 17
patient, el paciente, 11
paw, la pata, 20
peach, el durazno, 6
peacock, el pavo real, 20
peanuts, los cacahuates, 21
peas, los guisantes, 6
pedal, el pedal, 14
pedicurist, la pedicura, 12
pen, el bolígrafo, 1
pencil, el lápiz, 1
pencil sharpener, el sacapuntas, 1
penguin, el pingüino, 20
peninsula, la península, 32
people, las personas, 15
pepper, la pimienta, 10
petal, el pétalo, 5
pharmacist, la farmacéutica, 15
pharmacy, la farmacia, 8
phone booth, la cabina telefónica, 13
photo album, el álbum de fotos, 4
photograph, la fotografía, 4
photographer, el fotógrafo, 15
piano, el piano, 19
picnic, la excursión, 9
picture, el cuadro, 1
picture frame, el marco, 4
pie, la empanada, 6
pig, el cerdo, 9
piggy bank, la hucha, 13
piglet, el cochinillo, 9
pill, la pastilla, 11
pillow, la almohada, 2
pilot, el piloto, 17
pineapple, la piña, 6

pink, rosado, 28
plain, la llanura, 32
planet, el planeta, 23
plant, la planta, 1
plate, el plato, 10
play (a game), jugar, 27; (an instrument), tocar, 27
playground, el patio de recreo, 8
pliers, los alicates, 14
plumber, el plomero, 15
pocket, el bolsillo, 7
point (at), señalar, 27
polar bear, el oso polar, 20
police car, el coche de policía, 16
police station, la estación de policía, 8
policeman, el policía, 15
policewoman, la policía, 15
pond, el estanque, 9
ponytail, la cola de caballo, 12
popcorn, las palomitas, 21
porter, el mozo, 17
porthole, la portilla, 22
post office, el correo, 13
post-office box, el apartado postal, 13
postal worker, el empleado postal, 13
postcard, la tarjeta postal, 13
poster, el cartel, 2
postmark, el matasellos, 13
pot, el pote, 24
potato chips, las papas fritas a la inglesa, 6
potatoes, las papas, 6
potter, el alfarero, 24
powder, el polvo, 12
prepositions, preposiciones, 26
price, el precio, 6
prince, el príncipe, 25
princess, la princesa, 25
propeller, la hélice, 17
protractor, el prolongador, 1
pterodactyl, el pterodáctilo, 24
puddle, el charco, 5
pull, tirar, 27
pupil desk, el pupitre, 1
puppet, el títere, 4
puppy, el cachorro, 9
purple, morado, 28
purse, el bolso, 17
push, empujar, 27

queen, la reina, 25
quiver, la aljaba, 25

rabbit, el conejo, 9
race car, el coche de carreras, 14
racket, la raqueta, 18
radar screen, la pantalla de radar, 17
radio, el radio, 2
rag, el trapo, 14
rain, la lluvia, 5
rainbow, el arco iris, 5
raincoat, el impermeable, 7
raindrop, la gota de lluvia, 5
rake, el rastrillo, 5
raspberries, las frambuesas, 6
rat, la rata, 25
razor, la navaja de afeitar, 12
read, leer, 27
rearview mirror, el espejo retrovisor, 14
receive, recibir, 27
receptionist, la recepcionista, 13
record, el disco, 2
record player, el tocadiscos, 2
rectangle, el rectángulo, 30
red (hair), pelirrojo, 12; (color), rojo, 28
referee, el árbitro, 18
reflectors, los reflectores, 14
refrigerator, la nevera, 3
reins, las riendas, 25
reporter, el periodista, 15
rest rooms, los baños, 21
restaurant, el restaurante, 8, 10
return address, el remitente, 13
rhinoceros, el rinoceronte, 20

rice, el arroz, 10
ride a bicycle, montar en bicicleta, 27
right, derecho, 26
ring (jewelry), la sortija, 7; (circus), la pista de circo, 21
ringmaster, el maestro de ceremonias, 21
rings (planet), los anillos, 23
river, el río, 32
road, el camino, 9
roar, rugir, 27
robot, el robot, 23
rock, la piedra, 24
rocket, el cohete, 23
rocking chair, la mecedora, 2, 4
rocking horse, el caballo mecedor, 4
roller skates, los patines de ruedas, 16
roof, el tejado, 2
rooster, el gallo, 9
rope, la cuerda, 19, 21
rope ladder, la escalera de cuerda, 21
rowboat, el bote de remos, 16
rubber band, la cinta de goma, 13
rubber stamp, el sello de goma, 13
rug, la alfombra, 1
ruler, la regla, 1
run, correr, 27
running, el correr, 18
runway, la pista, 17
saber-toothed tiger, el tigre de dientes de sable, 24

sad, triste, 26
saddle, la silla de montar, 25
safe, la caja fuerte, 13
safety deposit box, la caja de seguridad, 13
safety net, la red de seguridad, 21
sail, la vela, 16
sailboat, el barco de vela, 16
sailing, la navegación, 18
sailor, el marinero, 15
salad, la ensalada, 10
salesman, el vendedor, 15
saleswoman, la vendedora, 15
salt, la sal, 10
sand, la arena, 22
sandals, las sandalias, 7
sandbox, el cajón de arena, 8
sandpaper, el papel de lija, 3
sandwich, el bocadillo, 10
satellite, el satélite, 23
saucer, el platillo, 10
sausages, las salchichas, 10
saw, la sierra, 3
saxophone, el saxofón, 19
scale, la báscula, 6; la balanza, 13
scales (fish), las escamas, 22
scarf, la bufanda, 7
scenery, el decorado, 19
school (for children), la escuela, 8; (of fish), el banco, 22
school bus, el autobús escolar, 16
scientist, el científico, 23
scissors, las tijeras, 1, 12
scooter, el patinete, 16
screw, el tornillo, 3
screwdriver, el destornillador, 3
script, el guión, 19
scuba diver, el buceador, 22
sea, el mar, 32
sea horse, el hipocampo, 22
sea turtle, la tortuga de mar, 22
sea urchin, el erizo marino, 22
seal, la foca, 20
seashell, la concha de mar, 22
seasons, las estaciones, 5
seat, el asiento, 17
seat belt, el cinturón de seguridad, 14
seaweed, el alga marina, 22
second, segundo, 31
secretary, la secretaria, 15
security camera, la cámara de seguridad, 13
security guard, el guardia de seguridad, 13
seesaw, el sube y baja, 8
sell, vender, 27

seven, siete, 31
seventeen, diecisiete, 31
seventh, séptimo, 31
seventy, setenta, 31
seventy-eight, setenta y ocho, 31
seventy-five, setenta y cinco, 31
seventy-four, setenta y cuatro, 31
seventy-nine, setenta y nueve, 31
seventy-one, setenta y uno, 31
seventy-seven, setenta y siete, 31
seventy-six, setenta y seis, 31
seventy-three, setenta y tres, 31
seventy-two, setenta y dos, 31
sewing machine, la máquina de coser, 19
shadow, la sombra, 9
shampoo, el champú, 12
shapes, las formas, 30
shark, el tiburón, 22
sharp, puntiagudo, 26
shaving cream, la crema de afeitar, 12
sheep, la oveja, 9
sheet, la sábana, 2
sheet music, la música, 19
shelf, el estante, 2
shield, el escudo, 25
shipwreck, el naufragio, 22
shirt, la camisa, 7
shoelace, el cordón, 7
shoes, los zapatos, 7
shopping bag, la bolsa de compras, 6
shopping cart, el carrito de compras, 6
short (not long), corto, 12, 26; (not tall), bajo, 26
shorts, los pantalones cortos, 7
shoulder, el hombro, 11
shovel, la pala, 5
shower, la ducha, 2
sidewalk, la acera, 16
sign (in a store), el letrero, 6; (traffic), la señal, 8
signature, la firma, 13
silver (metal), la plata, 22; (color), plateado, 28
sing, cantar, 27
singer, el cantante, 19
sink, el fregadero, 3
sister, la hermana, 29
sit down, sentarse, 27
six, seis, 31
sixteen, dieciséis, 31
sixth, sexto, 31
sixty, sesenta, 31
sixty-eight, sesenta y ocho, 31
sixty-five, sesenta y cinco, 31
sixty-four, sesenta y cuatro, 31
sixty-nine, sesenta y nueve, 31
sixty-one, sesenta y uno, 31
sixty-seven, sesenta y siete, 31
sixty-six, sesenta y seis, 31
sixty-three, sesenta y tres, 31
sixty-two, sesenta y dos, 31
skate, patinar, 27
skateboard, la tabla de patines, 16
skates, los patines, 18
skating, el patinaje, 18
skeleton, el esqueleto, 24
ski, esquiar, 27
skirt, la falda, 7
skis, los esquís, 18
sky, el cielo, 9
skydiving, el salto libre con paracaídas, 18
skyscraper, el rascacielos, 8
sled, el trineo, 5
sleep, dormir, 27
sleeping bag, el saco de dormir, 9
sleeve, la manga, 7
slide, el tobogán, 8
sling, el cabestrillo, 11
slow, despacio, 26
small, pequeño, 26
smile, la sonrisa, 11
smoke, el humo, 9
smokestack, la chimenea, 8
snack bar, la cafetería, 17
snake, la serpiente, 20
sneeze, el estornudo, 11
snorkel, el esnórquel, 22

slow, despacio, 26
small, pequeño, 26
smile, la sonrisa, 11
smoke, el humo, 9
smokestack, la chimenea, 8
snack bar, la cafetería, 17
snake, la serpiente, 20
sneeze, el estornudo, 11
snorkel, el esnórquel, 22
snow, la nieve, 5
snowball, la bola de nieve, 5
snowflake, el copo de nieve, 5
snowman, la figura de nieve, 5
snowmobile, el carro de nieve, 5
snowplow, la máquina barredora de nieve, 5
snowstorm, la tormenta de nieve, 5
soap, el jabón, 6
soccer, el fútbol, 18
soccer ball, la pelota (de fútbol), 18
socks, los calcetines, 7
sofa, el sofá, 2
soft, suave, 26
soft drink, el refresco, 10
solar panel, el tablero solar, 23
solar system, el sistema solar, 23
somersault, el salto mortal, 21
son, el hijo, 29
soup, la sopa, 10
south, sur, 32
South America, la América del Sur, 32
South Pole, el Polo Sur, 32
southeast, sudeste, 32
southwest, sudoeste, 32
space, el espacio, 23
space helmet, el casco espacial, 23
space shuttle, el vuelo espacial, 23
space station, la estación espacial, 23
space suit, el traje espacial, 23
space walk, el caminar en el espacio, 23
spaceship, el platillo volante, 23
spatula, la espátula, 3
spear, la lanza, 24
sphere, la esfera, 30
spider, la araña, 25
spiderweb, la telaraña, 25
spinach, las espinacas, 6
spinning wheel, el torno de hilar, 4
spokes, los rayos, 14
sponge, la esponja, 3
spoon, la cuchara, 10
sports, los deportes, 18
spotlight, el proyector de teatro, 19
spots, las manchas, 20
spring, la primavera, 5
sprinkler, la regadera, 5
square (park), la plaza, 8; (shape), el cuadrado, 30
squid, el calamar, 22
squire, el escudero, 25
stable, el establo, 25
stage, el escenario, 19
stairs, la escalera, 2
stamp, el sello, 13
stand up, ponerse de pie, 27
stapler, la grapadora, 1
staples, las grapas, 1
starfish, la estrella de mar, 22
stars, las estrellas, 23
statue, la estatua, 8
steak, el bistec, 10
steering wheel, el volante, 14
stem, el tallo, 5
stethoscope, el estetoscopio, 11
stick, el palo, 24
stilts, los zancos, 21
stingray, la pastinaca, 22
stirrup, el estribo, 25
Stop!, ¡Alto!, 16
stop sign, la señal de alto, 16
stove, la estufa, 3
straight, liso, 12
straw, la paja, 10
strawberries, las fresas, 6
street, la calle, 16
string, la cuerda, 4; el cordel, 13

strings, las cuerdas, 19
stripes, las rayas, 20
stroller, el cochecito de niño, 16
student (female), la alumna, 1; (male), el alumno, 1
submarine, el submarino, 22
suds, la espuma, 12
sugar, el azúcar, 10
suit, el traje, 7
suitcase, la maleta, 17
summer, el verano, 5
sun, el sol, 23
sunglasses, los anteojos de sol, 7
sunroof, el techo de sol, 14
supermarket, el supermercado, 6
swan, el cisne, 20
sweater, el suéter, 7
sweatpants, los pantalones de entrenamiento, 7
sweatshirt, la camisa de entrenamiento, 7
swim, nadar, 27
swimming, la natación, 18
swimming pool, la piscina, 18
swings, los columpios, 8
sword, la espada, 25
swordfish, el pez espada, 22

table, la mesa, 3
table tennis, el tenis de mesa, 18
tablecloth, el mantel, 10
tail, la cola, 20
tailor, el sastre, 15
take a bath, bañarse, 27
talent show, el espectáculo, 19
talk, hablar, 27
tall, alto, 26
tank truck, el camión tanque, 14
tape measure, la cinta para medir, 3
taxi, el taxi, 16
taxi driver, el taxista, 15
tea, el té, 10
teach, enseñar, 27
teacher (female), la maestra, 1; (male), el maestro, 1
teddy bear, el osito, 4
telephone, el teléfono, 2
television, la televisión, 2
television repairer, el reparador de televisión, 15
teller, la cajera, 13
ten, diez, 31
ten thousand, diez mil, 31
tennis, el tenis, 18
tennis racket, la raqueta de tenis, 17
tent, la tienda de campaña, 9
tent pole, el palo de tienda, 21
tentacle, el tentáculo, 22
tenth, décimo, 31
test tube, el tubo de ensayo, 23
thermometer, el termómetro, 11
thin, delgado, 26
think, pensar, 27
third, tercero, 31
thirteen, trece, 31
thirty, treinta, 31
thirty-eight, treinta y ocho, 31
thirty-five, treinta y cinco, 31
thirty-four, treinta y cuatro, 31
thirty-nine, treinta y nueve, 31
thirty-one, treinta y uno, 31
thirty-seven, treinta y siete, 31
thirty-six, treinta y seis, 31
thirty-three, treinta y tres, 31
thirty-two, treinta y dos, 31
thousand, mil, 31
three, tres, 31
throne, el trono, 25
throw, tirar, 27
thumb, el pulgar, 11
ticket (plane), el boleto, 17
ticket agent, el vendedor de boletos, 17
ticket booth, la taquilla, 21
ticket counter, el mostrador de boletos, 17
tickets (to the circus), las entradas, 21
tie, la corbata, 7

tiger, el tigre, 20
tiger cub, el cachorro de tigre, 20
tightrope, la cuerda floja, 21
tightrope walker, la gimnasta de la cuerda floja, 21
tights, el traje de malla, 7
tire, la llanta, 14
toast, la tostada, 10
toaster, el tostador, 3
toe, el dedo (del pie), 11
toenail, la uña (del pie), 12
toilet, el inodoro, 2
toilet paper, el papel higiénico, 2
tomatoes, los tomates, 6
tongue, la lengua, 11
toolbox, la caja de herramientas, 3
tooth, el diente, 11
toothbrush, el cepillo de dientes, 11
toothpaste, la pasta dentífrica, 11
top, de arriba, 26
top hat, el sombrero de copa, 4
tour guide, la guía, 15
tow truck, la grúa, 14
towel, la toalla, 2
tower, la torre, 25
toy soldiers, los soldados de juego, 4
toy store, la juguetería, 8
toys, los juguetes, 4
tractor, el tractor, 9
traffic jam, el embotellamiento de tráfico, 8
traffic lights, el semáforo, 8, 16
train, el tren, 16
train station, la estación del tren, 8
train tracks, las vías de ferrocarril, 9
training wheels, las ruedas de entrenamiento, 14
transportation, el transporte, 16
trapeze, el trapecio, 21
trapeze artist, el trapecista, 21
trash, la basura, 1
tray, la bandeja, 10
treasure, el tesoro, 22
treasure chest, el arca de tesoro, 22
tree, el árbol, 9, 24
triangle, el triángulo, 30
tricycle, el triciclo, 14
trombone, el trombón, 19
trophy, el trofeo, 18
truck, el camión, 16
truck driver, el camionero, 14
trumpet, la trompeta, 19
trunk (luggage), el baúl, 4, 14; (mammoth), la trompa, 24
T-shirt, la camiseta, 7
tuba, la tuba, 19
tugboat, el barco remolcador, 16
tundra, la tundra, 32
turban, el turbante, 21
turtle, la tortuga, 20
tusk, el colmillo, 24
tutu, el tutú, 19
tuxedo, el esmoquin, 4
twelve, doce, 31
twenty, veinte, 31
twenty-eight, veintiocho, 31
twenty-five, veinticinco, 31
twenty-four, veinticuatro, 31
twenty-nine, veintinueve, 31
twenty-one, veintiuno, 31
twenty-seven, veintisiete, 31
twenty-six, veintiséis, 31
twenty-three, veintitrés, 31
twenty-two, veintidós, 31
two, dos, 31
typewriter, la máquina de escribir, 13

umbrella, el paraguas, 4, 7
umpire, el árbitro, 18
uncle, el tío, 29
under, debajo de, 26
underwear, la ropa interior, 7
unicorn, el unicornio, 25
unicycle, el monociclo, 21
uniform, el uniforme, 4

video camera, la cámara de video, 17
videocassette player, el pasador de videos, 2
village, la villa, 24
violin, el violín, 19
volcano, el volcán, 32
volleyball, el voleibol, 18

wait, esperar, 27
Wait!, ¡Espere!, 16
waiter, el camarero, 10
waiting room, la sala de espera, 11
waitress, la camarera, 10
walk, caminar, 27
wall, la pared, 2
wallet, la billetera, 13
walrus, la morsa, 20
wash oneself, lavarse, 27
washing machine, la lavadora, 3
wastebasket, la papelera, 1
watch (for telling time), el reloj, 7; (verb), mirar, 27
water, el agua, 24; (verb), regar, 27
waterfall, la catarata, 32
watermelon, la sandía, 6
wave, la ola, 22

wavy, ondulado, 12
weather, el tiempo, 5
weather forecaster, el meteorólogo, 15
weaver, la tejedora, 24
weight lifting, el levantamiento de pesos, 18
well, el pozo, 24
west, oeste, 32
wet, mojado, 26
wet suit, el traje de goma, 22
whale, la ballena, 22
wheat, el trigo, 24
wheel, la rueda, 24
wheelchair, la silla de ruedas, 11
whip, el látigo, 21
whistle, el pito, 4
white, blanco, 28
wide, ancho, 26
wig, la peluca, 19
wind, el viento, 5
window, la ventana, 2
windshield, el parabrisas, 14
windshield wipers, los limpiaparabrisas, 14
wing, el ala, 17
wings, las alas, 20
winter, el invierno, 5
wolf, el lobo, 20

woman, la mujer, 9
wood, la madera, 3
words, las palabras, 27
worm, el gusano, 5
wrench, la llave de tuercas, 3
wrestling, la lucha libre, 18
write, escribir, 27

X ray, los rayos X, 11
xylophone, el xilófono, 19

yard, el patio, 5
yarn, el hilado, 4
yellow, amarillo, 28
yolk, la yema, 10

zebra, la cebra, 20
zero, cero, 31
zip code, el código postal, 13
zipper, la cremallera, 7
zoo, el jardín zoológico, 20
zookeeper, el guardián de zoológico, 20